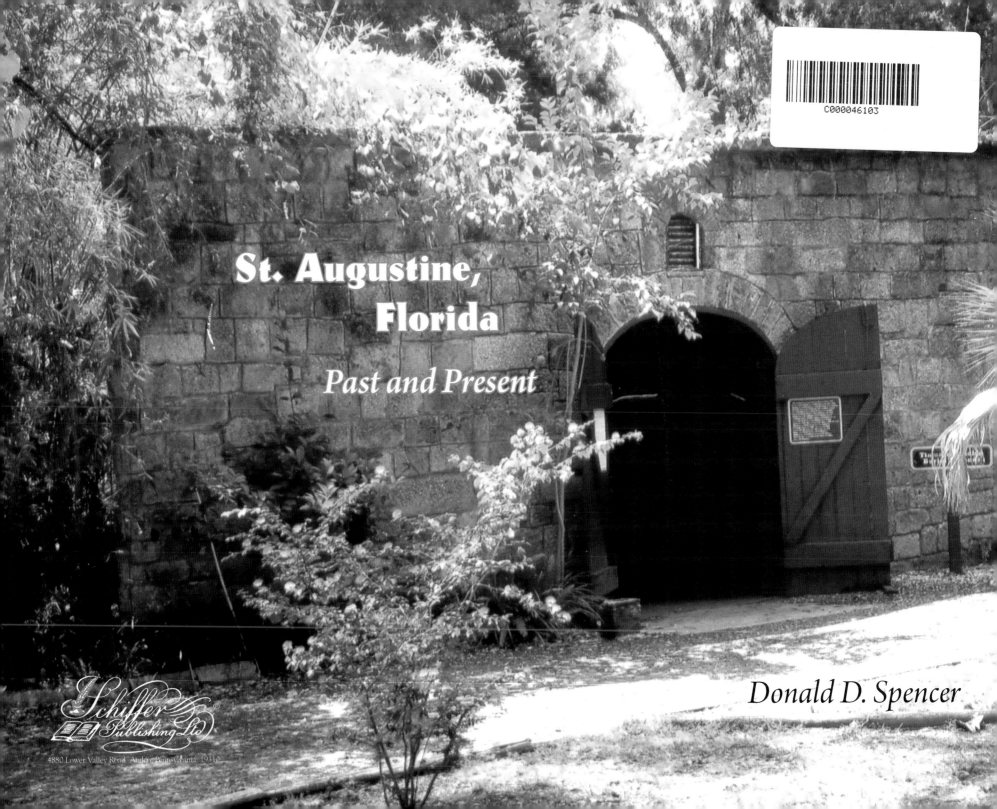

St. Augustine, Florida

Past and Present

Donald D. Spencer

Schiffer Publishing Ltd
4880 Lower Valley Road, Atglen, Pennsylvania 19310

C000046103

Drawings from Dover Publications, Inc., appear on pages 9, 12, and 18.

Dedication

For Sandra, Susan, Sherrie, Steven and Laura, whom I hope will develop an appreciation for the nation's oldest city, enhancing a love for their country.

Other Schiffer Books by Donald D. Spencer
Greetings from Daytona Beach, 978-0-7643-2806-0, $24.95
Greetings from Ormond Beach, 978-0-7643-2809-1, $24.95
Greetings from Tampa, 978-0-7643-2898-5, $24.95
Greetings from St. Augustine, 978-0-7643-2802-2, $24.95

Other Schiffer Books on Related Subjects
Greetings from St. Petersburg, 978-0-7643-2690-5, $24.95
St. Petersburg: Past and Present, 978-0-7643-2903-6, $24.95
Fort Lauderdale Memories, 978-0-7643-2828-2, $24.99

Copyright © 2009 by Donald D. Spencer
Library of Congress Control Number: 2008936720

All rights reserved. No part of this work may be reproduced or used in any form or by any means—graphic, electronic, or mechanical, including photocopying or information storage and retrieval systems—without written permission from the publisher.

The scanning, uploading and distribution of this book or any part thereof via the Internet or via any other means without the permission of the publisher is illegal and punishable by law. Please purchase only authorized editions and do not participate in or encourage the electronic piracy of copyrighted materials.

"Schiffer," "Schiffer Publishing Ltd. & Design," and the "Design of pen and ink well" are registered trademarks of Schiffer Publishing Ltd.

Designed by Stephanie Daugherty
Type set in Arno Pro /Souvenir Lt BT/
Humanista 521 BT

ISBN: 978-0-7643-3146-6
Printed in China

Schiffer Books are available at special discounts for bulk purchases for sales promotions or premiums. Special editions, including personalized covers, corporate imprints, and excerpts can be created in large quantities for special needs. For more information contact the publisher:

Published by Schiffer Publishing Ltd.
4880 Lower Valley Road
Atglen, PA 19310
Phone: (610) 593-1777
Fax: (610) 593-2002
E-mail: Info@schifferbooks.com

For the largest selection of fine reference books on this and related subjects, please visit our web site at:

www.schifferbooks.com

We are always looking for people to write books on new and related subjects. If you have an idea for a book please contact us at the above address. This book may be purchased from the publisher. Include $5.00 for shipping. Please try your bookstore first. You may write for a free catalog.

In Europe, Schiffer books are distributed by
Bushwood Books
6 Marksbury Ave.
Kew Gardens
Surrey TW9 4JF England
Phone: 44 (0) 20 8392-8585
Fax: 44 (0) 20 8392-9876
E-mail: info@bushwoodbooks.co.uk
Website: www.bushwoodbooks.co.uk

Free postage in the U.K., Europe; air mail at cost.

Contents

Ready to Write a Book?

Do you collect images of your town or county? Are you passionate about local history, and eager to share what you've learned? If you or your organization always dreamed of writing a book, we would love to hear from you. We are eagerly seeking authors to write illustrated, regional history and guide books. We'd love to hear more about the images you have access to, and the audience you are writing for.

Email your book idea to info@schifferbooks.com, write to Acquisitions, Schiffer Publishing, Ltd. 4880 Lower Valley Rd., Atglen, PA 19310 USA, or call 610-593-1777 to make an appointment to speak with an editor.

Preface

Just as history was punctuated with "essential moments"—brief battles that determined the destiny of nations, chance discoveries that commenced centuries of colonization—geography was interspersed with "essential places." These crucial locales were keystones in their regions, places through which supply reached demand, from which officialdom wielded power, to which the ambitious arrived to earn riches and the masses came to earn something.

St. Augustine is one such essential place. Here, on the Atlantic coast in northeast Florida, cultural and economic forces from vast geographic regions and scores of societies have synergized for over four hundred years to form an urban enclave that exports more memorable signatures of character than any other city in America. St. Augustine's architecture, festivity, food, historical sites, statues, and even its street names are recognized and embraced worldwide as treasured traditions and icons. All are products of this geographic concentration of activity into a single crux.

The neighborhoods, streets, and buildings of St. Augustine signify more than mortar and brick. *St. Augustine Past and Present* is a freeze frame of the living history and geography of this essential city. It is a historical geography of the ancient city told through time-sequenced postcard views and photographs spanning over one hundred years (circa 1893 to 2008). The postcards are from the collection of the author, and he also took the accompanying photographs. These comparison shots capture many of the changes that have occurred over time. Unfortunately, some structures have been lost to the ravages of time, nature, or "progress." Mercifully, many have been preserved here for posterity.

Arranged by geographical areas (Plaza, North of Plaza, South of Plaza, Northwest of Plaza, Southwest of Plaza, and Anastasia Island), the *Past and Present* views offer how much, and how little, the city has changed throughout the last century.

Greetings from St. Augustine

THE OLD FORT - LOOKOUT TOWER

THE OLDEST HOUSE

ALCAZAR HOTEL - LIGHTNER MUSEUM

PONCE DE LEON HOTEL

PLAZA AND SPANISH CATHEDRAL

The Nation's Oldest City.
The Spanish founded St. Augustine almost 450 years ago to protect the treasure fleets traveling from the New World to Spain. Circa 2007, $1-3.

A Brief History of the Postcard

Early Postcards

Postcards first appeared in Austria in 1869, and in England and France in 1870. These early European cards carried no images; only space on one side for an address, the reverse side was for a message. But they enjoyed an advantage over first-class letter mail; they could be mailed at a reduced rate of postage. The first picture postcards appeared in Germany in 1870. The United States began to issue picture postcards in 1873 in conjunction with the Columbian Exposition in Chicago. These were illustrations on government printed postal cards and on privately printed souvenir cards. On May 19, 1898, private printers were granted permission, by an act of congress, to print and sell cards that bore the inscription "Private Mailing Card." The government granted the use of the word POST CARD to private printers on December 4, 1901. In this era, private citizens began to take black and white photographs and have them printed on paper with postcard backs. These cards are commonly called Real Photo postcards.

Real Photo Postcards

It was in 1902 that Eastman Kodak marketed its postcard size photographic papers. They quickly followed with a folding camera (model No. 3A) that was specially designed for making Real Photo postcards. To make matters even simpler, an amateur photographer could mail the camera with exposed film to Eastman Kodak. They would develop and print the postcards and return them to the sender with a reloaded camera. These innovations in photography as applied to the postcard captured the public imagination. It had become possible for anyone who owned a camera to make personalized photo postcards.

Postcards Become Popular

The picture postcard did not come into common use in the United States until after 1900. It was about 1902 that the postcard craze hit the country and it was not long before a wide variety of printed postcards were available: advertising, expositions, political, greetings, and more. Collectors would send postcards to total strangers in faraway places, asking for local cards in return. Some collectors specialized in railroad depots, street scenes, cemeteries, churches, courthouses, farms, holidays, animals, military scenes, casinos, ethnic images, sports, hotels, transportation devices, parks, bathing beauties, industrial scenes, beach scenes, plants, lighthouses, restaurants, space, amusement parks, rivers, steamboats, plants, agricultural products, even comic cards; others collected anything they could find. Postcard albums, bought by the millions were filled with every sort of postcard ever issued. The craze was actually worldwide since many countries had postcards. Acceptance by the

Large Letter Postcard.
The Curt Teich & Co. near Chicago churned out more postcards than any other printer in the world. Over its eighty-year history, the company produced cards featuring more than 10,000 towns and cities in North America and eighty-seven foreign countries. Teich's Large Letter Postcards are especially popular with collectors. Circa 1940s, $3-5.

public was immediate and enthusiastic. Postcards afforded an easy means of communication. They were an early version of today's email, though slower, of course, relying as they did on mail service.

The Divided Back Postcards

Before March 1, 1907, it was illegal to write any message on the same side of the card as the address. For that reason the early postcards often have handwriting all over the sides of the picture, and sometimes right across it. Many an otherwise beautiful card was defaced in this way. When postcards first started to go through the mails, they were postmarked at the receiving post office as well as that of the sender, making it easy to see the time involved between post offices—sometimes remarkably brief! The volume of postcards was an important reason for discontinuing the unnecessary second marking about 1910. For years postcards cost only a nickel for six and the postage was a penny, right up to World War II.

The most popular American postcards up to World War I were those made in Germany from photographs supplied by American publishers. At the time of the postcard craze, of course, color photography was still something of a rarity and not commercially viable. For the color cards, black and white photos were touched up, hand-colored, and then generally reproduced by lithography. Lithography consists of transferring the image to a lithographic stone, offset to a rubber blanket, and then printed onto paper. The details in the German produced cards were extremely sharp, and the best of them technically have never been matched since.

The German postcard industry folded up in the summer of 1914, when the war struck Europe, and never revived. Postcards produced during the years 1907 and 1915 had a divided back: the address was to be written on the right side; the left side was for writing messages. Millions of postcards were published during these years. Postcard collectors have hailed these opening years of the twentieth century as the "Golden Age" of postcards. During the golden era of the picture postcard, billions of postcards rolled off the printing presses. In 1917 the United States entered World War I and the postcard craze ended.

White Border Postcards

With the advent of World War I, the supply of postcards for American consumption switched from Germany to England and the United States. Postcards printed in the United States during the years 1915-1930 were classified as White Border cards. To save ink, a colorless border was left around the view. These postcards were of a poorer quality as compared to the cards printed in Germany.

Linen Postcards

In 1930 the "linen" textured card was introduced and was popular until 1950. While this card was less expensive to produce, it reduced the clarity of detail in the pictures. These cheap cards are typically printed in vivid colors on paper with a crosshatched surface, which resembled linen fabric. "Linen" refers to the texture-like feel of the cardboard stock. The cards of this period romanticized the images of diners, gas stations, hotels, commercial buildings and tourist attractions. Using the photographic image of an establishment, all undesirable features, such as background clutter, people, telephone poles, and even cars were removed by airbrushing. World War II occupied most people's attention during much of this period, but the prosperity that followed soon was reflected in cards from communities all over the United States.

Photochrome Postcards

In 1950 the "photochrome" or "chrome" postcard with a glossy finish replaced the linen card This type of finish allowed for a very sharp reproduction of the picture, however, the cards seem to have lost much of both the role and nature of earlier cards. The chrome card, which is offered for sale today in gift shops, is where full-color photographic images are reproduced as a half tone on modern lithography presses. A varnish or lamination is applied on the card to give it a shiny look. In 1970, a king-sized chrome card (4.125-inch by 5.875-inch) was introduced and by 1978 it was in general use everywhere. This card is also called a continental or modern postcard.

Chapter One:

In the Beginning

History stretches back farther in St. Augustine than in any other continuously occupied city in the United States. This ancient city was founded before the English colonized Jamestown, Virginia, and fifty-five years before the Pilgrims landed at Plymouth Rock, Massachusetts. St. Augustine survives to preserve layer after layer of history and as a testament of how this nation was won, developed, and lives on.

Life in what is now Florida was quite different when the early Indian civilizations lived here. What we know about these people comes from studying artifacts—the man-made remains such as tools, weapons, clothing, skeletons, and bits of pottery. Archaeologists study artifacts and interpret clues about the way prehistoric people obtained food, how they ate, how they built houses, how they dressed, how they worshipped and how they battled enemy tribes.

Ancient Florida Indians

The Indians of Florida probably came across a land bridge that once connected Asia to Alaska, over what is now the Bering Strait. They may have followed animals southward, and slowly over thousands of years ventured into the area we know as Florida. They were all Mongoloid peoples and we refer to them as Paleo Indians, meaning old or ancient Indians.

The Paleo Indians killed mastodons, saber-toothed tigers, and other large animals. The Paleo hunters used stone-tipped spears to kill some of them and stampeded others into traps.

Most of the Paleo Indians became hunter-cultivators with strong family and tribal ties. They were all similar in appearance with bronze skin, strong arms and legs, wide skulls, high cheekbones and straight black hair.

Indians in the Archaic Periods that followed were less dependent on large animals. They killed small animals with darts and spears and gathered the produce of the land and sea.

The early Indians were hunters and nomadic wanderers. When they arrived at the St. Johns River around 5,000 B.C. they found enough food to remain in one area. They began constructing shelters for protection from the more dangerous animals. They found fallen trees and hollowed them out for dugout canoes. This allowed them to travel greater distances, faster. It helped spread their culture throughout the area.

The early Indians learned to use flint and make simple pottery. They learned that maize (corn) placed in the ground would grow more maize. This discovery changed these Indians from hunters to farmers. Now they could establish permanent villages.

A society began to develop as stronger men became chiefs and their children were prepared to succeed them. The growth of villages developed into tribes and families stayed together longer. This gave them protection. Sometime during the development of the tribes and villages, religion began to develop.

The Florida Indians built houses of materials found near their villages. The Indians in central and northern Florida were forest people. They had homes of wooden poles and logs, with roofs of grass or palm fronds. The Indians of southern Florida had few trees in their areas. They built their homes of mud and sand, with roofs of palmetto fronds.

Around 1500 there were probably more than 100,000 Indians in Florida. At about this time, people from Europe began coming to Florida. The arrival of the Europeans brought about many changes for the Florida Indians. There were many tribes and villages existing in Florida at the time of the earliest European contact. Most of the Florida tribes had very close connections

Timucua Indian Village.
Florida's first people used a system of interconnected waterways for travel and trade. Most large villages were located along inland watercourses or the coast. The dugout canoe that evolved to ply Florida waters could go places otherwise impossible to reach.

linguistically or otherwise, with certain major tribes such as Apalachee, Calusa, or Timucua. Many of them spoke Muskhogen, Hitchiti, or Timucuan.

Many of the early Indian tribes were very hostile to the Europeans who landed on their shores. Warfare was a common occurrence between the Indians and the visiting Europeans.

Florida Indians Before 1500

The Indians found by the Spaniards in Florida were a wild and savage people. Two of the tribes in southern Florida, the Tequesta and Calusa Indians, were similar to the warlike natives of the Bahama Islands. The Indians living in the north belonged to the Timucua and Apalachee tribes.

The Indians were tall, copper-colored people, with long, straight, coarse hair, high cheekbones, and black, deep-set eyes. The early Spanish explorers declared that the men they met were like giants in size, and so strong that they could shoot an arrow and drive it through a tree the size of a man's thigh.

They wore a kind of coarse cloth of Spanish moss and palmetto fiber, which comprised most of their clothing. The women wore mantles of this material fastened on the shoulder with the right arm out, and skirts fastened at the waist and hanging to the feet. The men wore mantles over the shoulder in the same way, with short tunics of deerskin dressed and colored. They loved display and wore ornaments of gold and of pearls. They must have gotten the gold from the Indians of the nearest gold regions, and the pearls from their own waters. Some of the Indians tattooed their skins.

Their dwellings were usually grouped together in

Catching Fish in Shallow Water.
The Timucua Indians were skilled in fishing. Fish were usually harpooned or caught in weirs made of reeds. Hand lines with sinker and baited hook were also used. Sinkers were made of shell and stone. The simplest hooks were gorges: short bone pins sharpened on both ends with a line tied to the middle of the pin. The pin was baited and, when swallowed by a fish, it wedged transversely in the fish's throat.

villages surrounded by a close wall of posts ten to twelve feet high. In the northern part of Florida and on the Gulf Coast these dwellings were often mere shelters of poles covered with woven mats. With some tribes the houses were very substantial. In certain villages near the Atlantic coast, all the houses, except the chief's were circular, having floors level with the ground. The chief's house was often on a mound, and was not circular.

The chief was always very powerful. When he died his son ruled in his place. The tribes that were governed by these chiefs were fierce, and war was their delight. Like other Indians, they fought in small bands, and their weapons were arrows, spears, and clubs. Warriors were proud of the number of scalps they could take. They would sometimes take prisoners. Some of these were put to torture and afterward killed, some were kept as slaves. Occasionally a prisoner who showed very great courage would be adopted into the tribe.

These Indians were skilled in hunting and fishing. With streams, lakes and coastal waters alive with fish, and the woods full of bears, deer, turkeys, and other game, they fared well. Tilling the soil in a simple way, they raised food crops twice a year. The principal tool was a kind of hoe made of a shell fastened to the end of a stick. This primitive tool allowed the Indians to produce corn, beans, squash, and other vegetables. When vegetables could no longer be had, there were nuts and roots to be found. Gourds were raised to furnish dishes and vessels for various uses. The Indians thought much of their tobacco, and smoked it in a long pipe made of a cane with an earthen cup at the end, much as pipes are made now.

There were a number of feasts, but two especially, during the year when they would gather on the highest ground near the villages and offer sacrifices of plants and honey. A festival was held at the time of the corn planting and another when the corn was ripe.

The Indians were grave, dignified people, who talked little and seldom smiled. Yet they had their amusements—games of ball, wrestling, running, and leaping matches—and their dances.

Medicine men, called juavas, were expected to have a cure for every ailment. They were treated with great respect at all times, and were always consulted when anything of importance to the tribe was to be decided.

They were a strange people too; very fierce, very cruel to their enemies, but very brave and faithful to those of their own tribe. The story of Juan Ortiz, who was captured and lived with the Indians for many years, as well as other stories of their history, shows that they were capable of a high sense of honor and noble conduct.

The land that is now northeast Florida was the land of the Timucua Indians.

Timucua Indian Warriors.
A sixteenth century ceremony held prior to going on the warpath against an enemy Indian tribe. The Timucua Indians, in northeast Florida, were a warlike and well organized military.

Timucua Indian Making A Canoe.
Dugout canoes were almost always made from hard yellow pine and were about fifteen feet long.. The oldest dugout canoe was simply a hollowed-out log. Later, canoes were hollowed out by fire.

Statues of Timucua Indians.
These statues of Timucua Indians are part of an early Indian exhibit at the Orange County Regional History Center in Orlando.

Ponce de Leon Claims Florida

Juan Ponce de Leon, an explorer and adventurer, arrived in America with Columbus on his second voyage in 1493. Ponce de Leon set foot on Florida on April 3, 1513, and claimed the land for Spain. Because the discovery had been on the Pascua Florida (Easter season) and the land bloomed luxuriantly, he named it Florida. Eight years after his landfall, Ponce de Leon died from an injury he had sustained in a battle against the Florida Indians. In addition to founding Florida, Ponce de Leon also discovered the Gulf Stream, the warm, fast-moving ocean current that flows the length of Florida, a few miles offshore, on its way to Europe. The stream provided an admirable shipping route for the Spanish galleons taking the plundered gold and silver of South America back home to Spain.

Timucua Indian Chief Oriba Statue.

This statue represents Chief Oriba who was Chieftain of the Timucua Indian Village of Seloy when Ponce de Leon discovered Florida in 1513. The Seloy Village was located where the Fountain of Youth Archeological Park is now. Oriba was a very big man and had a great influence on the relationships between the Spanish and Indians. The overall appearance of the chief was decorative with bright colors; some of which were produced by boiling certain plants and roots together, resulting in different colors. The red mulberry tree was commonly used. The chief and his wives painted their skin around their mouths blue and were tattooed on the legs and arms using blue, red, and black designs. Chief Oriba's statue is located in the Fountain of Youth Archeological Park.

Coming of the Spaniards.

In 1513, just twenty-one years after Columbus' discovery of the New World, the aging governor of Puerto Rico, Juan Ponce de Leon, landed on the East Coast and named the land Florida. In 1521 he returned to Florida, this time to colonize the new country, but hostile Calusia Indians drove the Spaniards back to their ships. Ponce received an arrow wound that proved fatal; he died in July 1521. In 1559 his remains were moved to San Juan, Puerto Rico where they now rest in the Cathedral of San Juan. Copyright 1908, $6-8.

The Discovery of Florida.

On March 27, 1513, Easter Sunday, Juan Ponce de Leon and his three ships, the *Santiago*, *San Cristobel*, and *Santa Maria De La Consolacion*, sighted an island and continued north until they anchored offshore on April 2. They came ashore on April 3. He thought he had discovered an island, which he named Florida, the flower.

Early Contact With Europeans

Some of the earliest contact between Europeans and Timucua Indians came in the early 1500s when Spanish conquistadors led armies of exploration through Florida. In 1528, Spanish explorer Panfilo Narvaez and his army of four hundred men and some horses marched through Florida. In 1539 Spanish explorer Hernando De Soto and his army marched through the heart of Timucua Indian territory. Some of their relations with Florida peoples were friendly, but most resulted in conflict. When conflict arose, battles were fought and both Spaniards and Floridians died. The Floridians suffered greater casualties, because the Spaniards had advantages the Floridians did not—horses, war dogs, and firearms.

The conquistador's entradas affected native Florida groups in other ways as well. All along the journey, the Spaniards captured Indians to act as bearers, to carry the supplies an army needed to survive. The Indians pressed into service as bearers were taken miles from their homes, and many died along the way. Moreover, because armies must live off the land, the Spaniards traded for or simply took food supplies. This left native populations with food shortages. So those Floridians not killed in battle, or captured and taken away, probably faced long periods of hunger and malnutrition after the Spaniards passed through. Thus weakened, they were vulnerable to the disasters to come—smallpox, measles, and other diseases that were brought over by the Spaniards. The diseases spread rapidly through native groups, and nearly everyone became sick, resulting in an epidemic. These diseases decimated Florida Indian communities.

The Spanish Treasure Ships.
From the early 1500s, Spanish galleons carried vast amounts of treasure across the Atlantic Ocean and past the Florida Coast to Spain. They were laden with gold, silver, jewels, and other riches. Six Spanish expeditions between 1513 and 1563 all failed to settle Florida. In 1564, the French established a fort and colony on the St. Johns River that threatened the Spanish treasure fleets that sailed along Florida's shoreline.

French Settle in Florida

In 1562, three French ships under the command of Admiral Jean Ribault, an ardent Protestant, explored the mouth of the St. Johns River, near what is now Jacksonville. Two years later, French explorer Rene de Laudonniere established Fort Caroline near the area that Ribault had explored.

The French colony at Fort Caroline, near the mouth of the St. Johns River, threatened Spain's treasure fleets that sailed along Florida's shorelines. As a result of this incursion into Florida, Spain's King Philip II sent Pedro Menendez, the country's most experienced admiral and governor of Florida, to explore and to colonize the area. King Philip also instructed him to drive out the French settlers.

French Explorers Land in Northeast Florida.
On June 22, 1564, Captain Rene de Laudonniere landed in Florida, along the River of May (St. Johns River), with three ships and two hundred French Huguenot (Protestant) noblemen, soldiers, and artisans. The adventurous men and women brought their fears, hopes, and dreams: Could they survive in this strange land? Would they discover the riches they imagined? The French found a site (St. Johns Bluff) for their settlement on June 30. Protected by a bluff commanding a river view, the spot offered fertile land, potable water, woodland fruits, building materials, and lots of fish. The French soldiers thought the ground defensible and its closeness to the sea afforded access for ships. Above all, the Timucua Indians seemed friendly and willing to help them in their new world.

Indians Greet French Explorers.
In 1562, French explorers, led by Jean Ribault, arrived in Florida and were greeted by Timucua Indians. Their efforts to colonize failed, but in 1564 another French expedition landed at the St. Johns River, where they built Fort Caroline.

French Explorers Build Fort Caroline.
Timucua Chief Saturiwa's men crafted a shelter (similar to the one shown), so that Saturiwa could sit and watch the colonists build their settlement. When the French requested help, Saturiwa sent eighty of his strongest men. The natives helped dig Fort Caroline's moat; they gathered palmetto leaves, weaving a thatch to cover the colonists' houses. The Timucua Indians gave of their bounty—gold and silver, jewelry, pearls, animal hides, and medicinal plants. In return, Saturiwa sought a war alliance to help his people. When the alliance never materialized, Timucua Indian assistance dwindled.

Replica of Fort Caroline.
The engraving of Fort Caroline by Theodore DeBry of Jacques LeMoyne's painting was used by the National Park Service in its construction of the "fort model" in 1964. The model, believed to be perhaps 2/3 the overall size of the original, was formally dedicated June 28, 1964, exactly four hundred years after Rene de Laudonniere's colonizing expedition in La Florida. Shown is a replica of the original fort overlooking the St. Johns River at Fort Caroline National Memorial.

Chapter Two:

The Founding of St. Augustine

On September 8, 1565, with banners flying, trumpets sounding, artillery booming, and six hundred voyagers cheering, Admiral Pedro Menendez set foot on the shores of St. Augustine. In honor of the Saint whose feast day it was when Menendez first sighted shore, he named the town St. Augustine.

One of Menendez's first tasks was to attack the French settlement. He captured Fort Caroline on September 20, killing some 140 Frenchmen. Menendez then fell upon a shipwrecked French force led by Ribault fourteen miles south of St. Augustine, at the south end of the Matanzas River. Nearly all the French soldiers, including Ribault, were slaughtered.

Pedro Menendez had succeeded in removing the French forces from the New World and had also saved Spanish Florida from foreign occupation. St. Augustine would become the oldest lasting settlement in the continental land where Alaska, Canada, and the United States now exist.

Menendez Removes the French from Florida.
Jean Ribault arrived at Fort Caroline August 28, 1565, with reinforcements for the failing colony. On his heels stood a Spanish flotilla bent on ejecting the French. Escaping capture, Ribault sailed south to destroy the Spanish. A violent storm wrecked his fleet. Assuming that Fort Caroline was now vulnerable, Spanish commander Pedro Menendez ordered an overland assault; a French traitor led five hundred Spaniards through jungle and swamp to capture the poorly guarded French colony. The Spaniards killed 143 French colonists, sparing seventy women and children. Rene de Laudonniere, Jacques LeMoyne, and about fifty others escaped into the woods and eventually back to France. Only one Spaniard died.

Pedro Menendez.
Admiral Pedro Menendez, Spanish conquistador, decimated the French settlement Fort Caroline, near present-day Jacksonville, and secured the safety of Spanish treasure fleets. He founded St. Augustine in 1565.

Reenactment of Menendez Landing, St. Augustine.
Spanish explorer Pedro Menendez landed in Florida August 28, 1565 and established St. Augustine, the first permanent settlement in the U.S.

Pedro Menendez Statue.
A bronze statue dedicated to St. Augustine's founding father, Pedro Menendez, is in the front garden of the courtyard at Lightner Museum. Erected in 1972, it was presented to the city by Mayor Fernando Juarez of Aviles, Spain, which is St. Augustine's sister city. In 1979, the garden was formally dedicated as the Parque de Menendez.

Building St. Augustine.
Pedro Menendez and his men made friends with the Timucua Indians, moved into the "great house" of their village, built a moated fortification, and mounted four brass cannons. This view is from an art painting created for the American Oil Company. Circa 1950s, $4-6.

St. Augustine Site

When Pedro Menendez first arrived in the area where he established St. Augustine, he saw fires on the shore tended by Timucua Indians. These Indians were from the village whose cacique was named Seloy. Little is known about the village, but all references to it place its location as just north of St. Augustine and the mission Nombre de Dios, near the junction of the Tolomato and Matanzas Rivers. The village itself, through the hospitality of Seloy, became the first settlement of St. Augustine when Menendez's men fortified the large house and occupied the other houses for a short time.

Conflict with the Timucua Indians of Seloy forced the Spaniards to abandon the first settlement after a year and reestablish their town in its present location. Those Indians who chose to live in proximity of the town remained in small villages, just outside the walls of St. Augustine. Over the centuries there were always between two and ten of these villages within two miles of the town. In 1711 the Indian population around St. Augustine was 401, in 1717 the population had risen to more than 950, and in 1727 the population included 1350 Indians. After this time, however, the Indians in the St. Augustine vicinity began a rapid decline. In 1736 only 466 Indians were counted, and by 1752 there were only 150 adults in five villages. At the time of Spanish departure in 1763, there were just 86 Indians left in St. Augustine.

Timucua Indians reoccupied their Seloy village after the Spanish moved out and were joined by other groups who wanted to be near the mission and the protection of the Spanish town.

In 1934 a historic period Indian cemetery was discovered where the Fountain of Youth Park is today. Excavation of more than one hundred burials took place this year and was followed in 1935 by another exploratory excavation. The exposed burials were later recovered with earth and the site enclosed in a building for display. Excavations of the historic period Timucua Indian village associated with the burials began in 1950 and continued, at different times, in following years, providing much information about the Indians who lived in the Seloy village.

Spanish Missions

Spain consolidated her dominion over Florida through conversion of Native Indians to Christianity. Northward and westward of St. Augustine, missions reached into the most populace areas of aboriginal habitation. A mission, Nombre de Dios (Name of God), was established at the point of Menendez's landing. Following the establishment of the early Florida missions, more permanent missions were built in the Far West and California. Soon mission trails from St. Augustine to San Diego bridged the continent.

The First Mass in St. Augustine.
This diorama, on view in the Museum Building at the Mission of Nombre de Dios and the Shrine of Our Lady of La Leche, shows Father Lopez, a Spanish diocesan missionary priest, offering the first parish Mass in the United States, September 8, 1565. Pedro Menendez and his crew surround the altar and St. Augustine, Florida, our nation's oldest city, is founded. Circa 1940s, $1-3.

Pirates Attack St. Augustine

English commander Sir Francis Drake wrecked havoc on the Spanish ships and settlements in the new world. The Spanish called him a pirate, but the English had another name for him—a privateer. Whether someone was a pirate or a privateer depended on who was doing the name-calling. The word "pirate" comes from a Greek word, peiran, which means "to attack" and was used for any brigand who illegally attacked ships. The English word also comes from the Latin pirata, "one who plunders or robs on the sea." Nations used the term "pirate" for someone from another nation who attacked their ships. A privateer, on the other hand, was someone who had official papers from his government that allowed him to attack and capture enemy ships.

Sir Francis Drake (1540-1596).
Sir Francis Drake was a British pirate and privateer whose success at plundering Spanish ships in the New World made both him and the English queen, Elizabeth I, very rich. He was the first Englishman to circumnavigate the globe and was knighted in 1581. In June 1586, Drake led an English fleet of 2,000 men in attack against St. Augustine. When the raiders had departed after sacking and burning the city, the Spanish began the task of rebuilding.

Pirates Attack St. Augustine.
Pirates had a reputation for cruelty that many lived up to. They knew their victims would surrender more easily if resistance were punished with torture and death. In 1668 the pirate John Davis and his English buccaneers landed in St. Augustine and killed sixty Spaniards. The wooden fort withstood the pirate assault, but the town was plundered. The constant threat from pirates, and the growing menace of the English in Carolina, prompted Spain to build of a stone fort.

Pirates.
Pirates—Were they robbers at sea? Daring figures that swooped down on treasure ships and remote cities and returned home with golden cargoes? Brutal sea thieves who showed no mercy to their victims? Bold adventurers who financed travel by nautical theft? They were all these and more.

In 1567, Francis Drake joined English pirate Sir John Hawkins, his cousin, and a Caribbean slave runner while a 22-year-old captain of his own vessel, the *Judith*. Their voyage ended in disaster as the Spanish destroyed several vessels in the fleet and almost captured Hawkins and Drake. This started Drakes' life-long personal war with Spain. In 1586, Drake attacked and burned St. Augustine.

The Spanish rebuilt, but eighty-two years later, in 1668, the English pirate Captain Robert Searles, alias John Davis, attacked St. Augustine. Searles and his men looted homes and stores and ended up killing some sixty Spaniards, nearly one-fourth of the total population of Florida.

Building of the Castillo

Following the second attack by pirates, Don Manuel de Cendoya, governor of Florida, began building Castillo de San Marcos, one of the greatest of the great system of Spanish fortifications at key points in this hemisphere. Building the main part of the great fort took a quarter-century, and during the next hundred years St. Augustine's history was largely centered on the Castillo.

The fort was built between the years 1672 and 1695. In 1702 James Moore, the British Governor of South Carolina and a force of 800 men marched on St Augustine, quickly capturing the town and surrounding the fort. All the city's residents were huddled inside the Castillo. They besieged the fort, but their guns failed to breach the walls. On withdrawal they burned St. Augustine, and once more the residents began rebuilding as best they could.

This was the second burning of St. Augustine by an enemy. The colonists, determined to make the city safe, built walls, earthworks and redoubts around the entire settlement. Thus all of St. Augustine became a fortress with the Castillo guarding the key position. This rebuilding was finished just in time for St. Augustine's most thorough baptism of fire by an enemy.

England's Oglethorpe Attacks St. Augustine

In 1740, General James E. Oglethorpe, governor of Georgia, with a fleet of thirteen vessels and nine hundred men, attacked St. Augustine. However, Colonel Manuel de Montiano, the Spanish governor in St. Augustine, was ready with 750 men and four small, but fast, ships.

Castillo de San Marcos.
The year 1672 saw work begun on the stone fortress called Castillo de San Marcos. The fort, though nearly completed in 1696, was not officially dedicated until 1756. The strength of the fort was proven in 1702, when Governor James Moore of Carolina led a two-month siege without success, and in 1740, an even stronger attack by British General James Oglethorpe of Georgia was turned away.

The British cannon balls and shots failed to dent the Castillo de San Marcos fort. General Oglethorpe's next move was to shell the town to try to panic the civilians into appealing for surrender or driving them into the fort. But instead of moving into the Castillo where two thousand extra people would complicate the firing, the citizens simply moved out of firing range.

Oglethorpe then tried a blockade to starve both the townspeople and the soldiers. However, five supply ships from Cuba managed to supply food to the citizens and soldiers of St. Augustine.

After thirty-eight days of siege, General Oglethorpe, who had sworn "to take St. Augustine or leave his bones before its walls," did neither. The frustrated British forces left Florida and went home.

20

CASTILLO DE SAN MARCOS, ST. AUGUSTINE

Fort Names.
Spanish soldiers occupied Castillo de San Marcos during the years 1696-1763 and 1783-1821. During the short British occupation of Florida, 1763-1783, the fort was called Fort St. Marks. Eventually the Castillo and Florida came into American hands through a treaty signed in 1821. In 1824 Congress ordered the name of the Castillo changed to Fort Marion, but, in 1942, restored its original Spanish name, Castillo de San Marcos—this nation's oldest masonry fortification. Circa 2008, $1-3.

Cubo Line.
A log wall called the Cubo Line was built in 1808 on the site of earlier earthworks. This line reached from the Castillo de San Marcos on Matanzas Bay to San Sebastian River, thus barring land approach to St. Augustine. Needle-sharp Spanish bayonet plants at the foot of the wall helped to make it a formidable defense.

Fort Matanzas.
Fort Matanzas was located sixteen miles to the south of St. Augustine. It guarded the lower entrance to St. Augustine's harbor. Fort Matanzas was erected in 1740-1742. Circa 2000, $1-3.

Chapter Three:
Battle for Control of Florida

English Control of Florida (1763-1783)

As a result of the Treaty of 1763, which established peace between Spain and England at the conclusion of the Seven Years War, Florida was ceded to the English in exchange for Havana, Cuba, which had been taken by an English fleet during the war. This cession was very distasteful to the Floridians, and nearly of them relocated to Mexico and the West Indies.

For the next twenty years, England owned the old colony and divided it into two new provinces: East Florida and West Florida. St. Augustine continued as the capital of East Florida. English soldiers and subjects ultimately moved into the community bring colonists from the Mediterranean islands with them. St. Augustine soon became a multi-cultural and multi-national community. The transfer of St. Augustine and Florida from Spanish to British rule in 1763 resulted in religious change as well; Spanish Catholicism was replaced by English Protestantism, except for many Minorcans who continued as practicing Catholics in the old colony.

During the British occupation of Florida, there was widespread colonial development. Large plantations turned St. Augustine into a commercial seaport and encouraged much new permanent population.

Spanish Regains Control of Florida (1783-1821)

A Second Spanish Period followed the brief British Period of Florida history as a result of Spain's involvement in the American Revolutionary War. For almost forty years (1783-1821), Spaniards once again occupied St. Augustine and attempted to return its culture and Catholic religion to the colony. However, problems with a multi-cultural population mixture made Spain's second stay in Florida a difficult and exasperating endeavor. Finally Spain relinquished Florida with all of its difficulties to the United States. In return, the United States assumed responsibility for $5 million in claims of American citizens against Spain. The international agreement ended European control of St. Augustine and the old colony.

St. Augustine Changes Hands.
St. Augustine and Florida came into American hands through a treaty signed with Spain in 1821. On July 10, the Spanish flag came down for the last time, and the twenty-three starred flag of the United States rose over Castillo de San Marcos, shown in the background. Circa 1940s, $6-8.

St. Augustine in the 1800s

The city of St. Augustine was 256 years old as the United States formally took possession of the province of East Florida. And, on July 10, 1821, the Spaniards lowered the Spanish flag from atop the Castillo de San Marcos and then watched as the Stars and Stripes replaced their standard accompanied by cannon salutes. The Americanization of St. Augustine soon produced population growth and economic development.

St. Augustine served as an army base during the Second Seminole Indian War (1835-1842). Several Seminole warriors and two leaders, Osceola and Coacoochee, were imprisoned in the Castillo de San Marcos, then called Fort Marion, following their capture.

During the long and cruel Civil War conflict (1862-1865), St. Augustine was occupied by Union troops. Few military incidents took place in this portion of Florida and the community's citizens were spared the terrible suffering which so much of the South experienced for four years. As the Civil War ceased in 1865, St. Augustine was 300 years old.

Osceola.
A history of St. Augustine would be incomplete without mention of Osceola, a famed leader of the Seminole Indians. During the years 1835-1837 the United States fought a costly war in Florida with the Seminole Indians under the leadership of Osceola. In 1837 Osceola and a number of his warriors were captured a few miles south of St. Augustine and imprisoned in Fort Marian (Castillo de San Marcos). Osceola languished in captivity and died the following year at Fort Moultrie, South Carolina. The Second Seminole War dragged on until 1842. Today the descendants of the Seminoles who fought in the war still live in South Florida.

Slaves Freed

In January of 1863, President Abraham Lincoln's Emancipation Proclamation was officially issued in Florida at a St. Augustine site that is presently located as part of the Dow Museum of Historic Homes (was Old St. Augustine Village). A metal marker indicates the site. This action freed all slaves in Florida. Former St. Augustine slave Mary Gomez reported that when word of the Emancipation Proclamation reached the city, all slaveholders were ordered to release their slaves and allow them to gather in a large vacant lot at the Dow Museum of Historic Homes site. The slaves were freed during the reading and the "bonds" of the slaves, including Mary Gomez, were "struck off."

St. Augustine Lighthouse.
St. Augustine's Inlet to the sea was treacherous. Its shifting sands, called "crazy banks," were the dread of all who sailed to the ancient city. The St. Augustine Lighthouse, with its black and white spirals, was built in 1874, replacing the original coquina tower that was destroyed by the sea. For more than a century now, this spiral-striped tower has been an unforgettable landmark for visitors by land and sea. The light remains active and is visible from twenty miles away. Circa 2004, $1-3.

Military Cemetery.

The dead from Major Dade's detachment during the Second Seminole War (1835-1842) were buried on the battlefield, but seven years later, their remains were relocated to the National Cemetery in St. Augustine where a memorial now stands. The National Cemetery is Florida's oldest national military burial ground. Cancelled 1910, $5-7.

Tolomato Cemetery.

A map of the city of St. Augustine dated May 15, 1737, describes the site of Tolomato Cemetery as the "church and village of Tolomato, an Indian village served by the Franciscan Priests." The church was built of wood, but had a four-story coquina stone Belltower. When Florida was turned over to the British in 1763, the Spaniards and the Indians left with their Priests. Tolomato Church was torn down by the British troops for firewood, but the tower survived until the 1790s when, it is traditionally believed, the stones were used in the construction of the present Cathedral. The Christian Tolomato Indians buried their dead near the church and village.

The Roman Catholic Cathedral and Plaza.

Catholic Cathedral and Plaza de la Constitution.

This historic structure represents the original Catholic Church dedicated in 1797. It became a cathedral in 1870. Circa 1930s, $1-3.

Genoply House.

Juan Genoply, a Greek carpenter, built the Genoply House around 1788. It's the only surviving Second Spanish Period (1783-1821) frame building in the old city. The house was later used for educational purposes and is now known as the Oldest Wooden Schoolhouse. The Genoply House is on the left of this St. George Street scene. The City Gate is shown in the distance. Circa 1920s, $3-5.

Sequi-Kirby Smith House.

The Sequi-Kirby Smith House is one of only thirty Spanish Colonial houses remaining in St. Augustine. The house dates from the late 1700s. The site on which it's situated has been continuously occupied since the late 1500s. In 1786 it became the home of Bernardo Sequi, a prosperous merchant of Minorcan descent who was also baker to the garrison and a Spanish militia official. Judge Joseph Lee Smith, first Judge of the Superior Court for East Florida, rented the home around 1823 from Sequi's heirs, and in time the family purchased it. Edmund Kirby Smith was born in this house in May 1824. A West Point graduate, he became, at age 38, the

youngest lieutenant general in the Confederate Army and was the last Confederate general to surrender his command.

When General Smith and his sister sold the home in 1887, it became a boarding house with offices. In 1895 John L. and Frances Wilson gave the lot and building in trust to a private organization for use as a free public library. Today, the St. Augustine Historical Society holds the property under this trust as its historical research library. The "Sons of St. Augustine" statue is located in the courtyard of the Sequi-Kirby Smith House. On the left is Alexander H. Darnes, MD, (ca. 1840-1894) and on the right, Professor Edmund Kirby Smith (1824-1893). The St. Augustine Historical Society Research Library is open to the public.

Flagler Memorial Presbyterian Church.
Henry Flagler, builder of Florida's East Coast, erected this inspiring example of Venetian Renaissance architecture in 1889 as a memorial to his daughter. Flagler and members of his family lie in the mausoleum of Italian marble. Circa 1902, $3-5.

Ponce de Leon Hotel.
In 1888, Henry Flagler built a resort hotel in St. Augustine that rivaled the best hotels in the world. Many important visitors climbed the steps to the Ponce including five U.S. Presidents. Circa 1907, $6-8.

The Henry Flagler Era (1883-1899)

After the Civil War, millionaire Henry M. Flagler, co-founder of the Standard Oil Company, arrived with his railroad and grand ideas of making St. Augustine a winter haven for the northern rich. Flagler financed the economic development of the city and created the great "Gilded Age" empire of hotels and railroads that extended from St. Augustine south to Key West.

In St. Augustine, "Spanish Renaissance Revival" became the architectural form for Flagler's giant structures. Such a style featured clay-tile roofs, towers, rounded arches and extensive red terracotta ornamentation as well as poured concrete building supports and walls. Within ten years, the city of St. Augustine, known as the "Newport of the South," seemed full of winter homes, churches, and huge hotels mainly constructed in the Spanish Renaissance architectural style. The Ponce de Leon Hotel, opened in 1888, may never again be equaled for pure ornate splendor. It still stands today, now functioning as Flagler College.

Henry M. Flagler.
In 1883, Henry Morrison Flagler, a retired Standard Oil Company executive, was visiting Florida on a holiday and realized that better transportation facilities were needed. From that point on, until his death in 1913, he helped develop the East Coast of Florida, building a railroad line, the Florida East Coast Railway, from Jacksonville to Key West, and along the way, developed a number of grand hotels that catered to wealthy tourists. His hotel chain started with the Ponce de Leon, Alcazar, and Cordova hotels in St. Augustine. A reporter once asked John D. Rockefeller if he had conceived the idea of Standard Oil. "No, sir," replied the billionaire. "I wish I'd had the brains to think of it. It was Henry M. Flagler."

In the late nineteenth century, St. Augustine, as Flagler anticipated, became a refuge for rich Americans from the season of cold, winter northern cities. Once Flagler's Florida East Coast Railway was operational, northern visitors could reach the city in less than two days aboard comfortable trains with Pullman "Sleeping Cars." As a consequence, many celebrities came south to St. Augustine including John D. Rockefeller, Theodore Roosevelt, Will Rogers, William Harding and John Astor. Altogether, five United States Presidents stayed at the Ponce de Leon Hotel in the late nineteenth and early twentieth centuries.

This "golden era" ended in the early 1900s, as Flagler's interests moved south.

Twentieth Century and Beyond

In 1913, Henry M. Flagler died and was entombed in the mausoleum adjoining the Presbyterian Memorial Church in St. Augustine, where other members of his family already laid. St. Augustine reaped the benefits of Flagler's mighty empire. His buildings grace St. Augustine as both monuments and architectural gems.

Tourism and settlement soon changed St. Augustine and the entire state of Florida. In time, many northerners purchased property and settled in Florida, some on a seasonal schedule and others permanently. After World War I, middle class visitors also came south to the "Sunshine State" for their vacations. And, many of the visitors made plans for permanent settlement in Florida. St. Augustine became a popular place for visitors to experience and enjoy. By 1965, when St. Augustine celebrated its four hundredth birthday, the city was well known throughout America for its age and historical significance, unusual architecture, scenic beauty and entertaining activities.

St. Augustine stands today truly as a tribute to the past. Its "living history" includes: pre-historic and sixteenth century archeological remains; a seventeenth century Spanish fort; eighteenth century buildings; the sprawling giant Flagler structures of the nineteenth century; a nineteenth century alligator farm; and many twentieth century structures and businesses. Its historical literature is full of exciting events and famous personalities.

What future history will be made in this Ancient City is a question no one can answer. Perhaps it will not be as thrilling as the stories of old Spanish days, but one thing for sure: St. Augustine will make history by preserving the history she has!

With 120 pairs of matching vintage postcard views and contemporary photographs, *St. Augustine Past and Present* takes the reader on a journey through time. The vintage postcards of St. Augustine views, from the author's postcard collection, have been re-photographed from, in most cases, the same vantage point. The monetary values of the postcards shown in this book are provided as a guideline for collectors. The values are based upon the rarity of the postcard scenes. Condition has not been factored in and should be considered when evaluating individual postcards.

G 15027 The Sea Wall and Bath House, St. Augustine, Fla.

Feb 25/09

Will sail to day on "Comanche" at noon.

H.

Sea Wall.

From 1836-1842, the government reconstructed the Sea Wall that was originally built by the Spanish in 1690. It extends from the Castillo de San Marcos (Fort Marion) to the St. Francis Barracks. Shown in this view are the Sea Wall and Bath House. Cancelled 1909, $5-7.

Horse-drawn Tram.
Visitors to North Beach traveled one-third of a mile from Matanzas River to the Atlantic Ocean aboard horse-drawn trams. No charge was made for its use and the proceeds from the sale of this postcard were used for its upkeep. Note the horse pulling the train from the side and not from the front. Circa 1915, $10-12.

Shrimping Industry.
Shrimping played an important part as an industry in St. Augustine; this popular seafood was plentiful in local waters. The pot-bellied boats of the shrimp fleet were docked south of King Street on the San Sebastian River. The fleet comprised approximately 120 Diesel-powered boats ranging from fifty to seventy-five feet in length. Manned by Italian, Scandinavian, Spanish, Portuguese, and African-American crews, the vessels often remained at sea for days. The shrimping industry employed around 2,000 workers. The local industry quickly grew and by 1916 there were some thirty-two raw shrimp houses, ten canneries, and many small boats pulling some type of shrimping net to meet the growing demand of this specialty food. Today the shrimp boat docks are located on the San Sebastion River south of King Street on Riberia Street. Circa 1940s, $3-5.

Bridge of Lions.
An aerial view of Castillo de San Marcos, several shrimp boats, and the Bridge of Lions crossing the Matanzas River. Circa 1945, $1-3.

Ponce de Leon Celebration.
An annual Ponce de Leon celebration was held along the downtown waterfront and drew large crowds. These celebrations began in the 1880s and continued until the early 1930s. Circa 1910, $7-9.

Fountain of Youth Archaeological Park.
The location of the Fountain of Youth has archeological significance, both as the site of the ancient Indian town Seloy and a possible location where Ponce de Leon came ashore and established the Spain's claim to all of North America. Circa 1930s, $1-3.

Villa Zorayda.
Enchanted palace of the Moors; architect Franklin Smith designed the building in 1883 as his private home, reproducing a portion of the famed Alhambra in Spain. It's now a museum containing rare oriental art treasures collected by the late A. S. Mussallem. Circa 1940s, $2-4.

Casper's Ostrich and Alligator Farm.
In 1946, James Casper opened an attraction called Casper's Ostrich and Alligator Farm two miles north of downtown St. Augustine on U.S. Highway 1. There he raised alligators, crocodiles, ostriches, rare birds, and other animals. The roadside attraction later became the Gatorland Alligator Farm that operated until 1982. Circa 1946, $3-5.

Mill Wheel, 19 St. George Street.
This overshot wheel was powered by an artesian water well that ran from a gristmill on the second floor of what is now Milltop Tavern. Originally built in 1930 for Walter B. Fraser, it was rebuilt in 1947, and reconstructed in 1996 for J. R. Fraser.

Houses of St. Augustine.
When the Pilgrims landed at Plymouth Rock, St. Augustine was already a half-century-old. Founded in 1565, the city has been continuously inhabited ever since, with many structures that express the architectural styles of over four centuries of Spanish, British, and American rule. There are many coquina stone structures of colonial times, Victorian gingerbread homes, and structures of Spanish revival architecture still standing in St. Augustine. The home shown, 268 St. George Street, was designed in the Queen Anne Victorian style. Built in 1893 by Colonel John J. Upham, it's listed on the National Register of Historic Places. Referenced in books, the home is commonly known as the "Upham Winter Cottage."

David.
An exact replica of Michelangelo's "David," an eighteen-foot tall hand-carved marble statue weighing 20,000 pounds, stands at Ripley's Believe It Or Not! Museum—a rare, precise replica of the astonishing and sometimes controversial original. This statue is one of only two in the world carved as the original was: from a solid piece of pure Carrara Marble quarried from Pietra Santa in Tuscany, Italy, the same quarry where Michelangelo acquired the marble for his masterpiece. Michelangelo's original is housed in The Gallery of the Accademia di Belle Arti in Florence, Italy. David Sollazzini and Sons, of Italy, created this reproduction in 1962 for the World's Fair in 1963. Ripley's Museum obtained it in 2007.

St. Augustine Statues.

Hidden treasures are located throughout St. Augustine. Many "works of art" are incorporated into the buildings and grounds of, with statues and fountains located all over the ancient city. Besides the statues of Ponce de Leon, Pedro Menendez, and Henry Flagler, there are a variety of statues that one would expect to find in European cities.

Alligator Border Cards.
Early in the twentieth century the S. Langsdorff & Co. of New York published a series of 165 Florida postcards called the Alligator Border Series. These cards, printed in Germany, featured a trio of smiling alligators surrounding a different Florida image from Miami, Key West, Palm Beach, Palatka, St. Augustine, Tampa, Jacksonville, Ormond, Daytona, and miscellaneous topic images. Sixteen of the images were from the St. Augustine area. The printing and color quality of these postcards are exceptional. Alligator Border Cards are in great demand by present-day postcard collectors. This postcard scene is titled, "The Plaza." The Plaza de la Constitution is a landscaped parkway in the center of St. Augustine. The Constitution Monument and the Cordova Hotel can be seen in this view. Circa 1910, $30-100.

Alcazar Hotel and Cordova Annex.
Several horse-drawn carriages are shown in front of the Alcazar Hotel. The Cordova Hotel annex is on the left. Circa 1910, $40-100.

Ponce de Leon Hotel.
Henry Flagler's Ponce de Leon Hotel, as seen from across the street at the Alcazar Hotel. Circa 1910, $30-100.

Chapter Four

Around the Plaza

Constitution Monument, 1898.
The Constitution Monument is located at the west end of the Plaza de la Constitution in downtown St. Augustine. It was constructed in 1813, during the Second Spanish Period (1783-1821), to celebrate a newly formed constitutional government in Spain. The Spanish Parliament issued a royal decree that all plazas throughout the empire must construct commemorative monuments. The monument in St. Augustine is one of a few such commemorative structures remaining in the New World. It is also one of the oldest public monuments in the United States. The constitution was revoked in 1814, but colonists did not destroy this monument.

Constitution Monument, 2008.
The thirty-foot tall obelisk is constructed of smoothly plastered coquina. Marble plaques on each side read "Plaza de la Constitution." In 2001 the city of St. Augustine restored the masonry obelisk. Shown in the background of this view is the Government House Museum.

Government House, 48 King Street, Circa 1908.

Gonzalo Mendez de Canzo constructed a building in 1597-1603 that the King of Spain purchased in 1603, at a cost of 1,000 ducats, as a dwelling for the Governor of Florida. From that time on it was officially recognized and known as the Governor's Mansion. Since the 1600s a succession of governor's houses have stood at the west end of the Plaza de la Constitution. In 1834 St. Augustine's new owner, the United States, drastically renovated what was then called Government House. Robert Mills (1781-1855), a United States architect and the designer of the Washington Monument, drew the plans for the building, retaining parts of the earlier walls. This building housed the post office, public library, courthouse, and other Federal offices. The cannon shown in this view is in the Plaza de la Constitution, across the street. ($8-10.)

Government House, 48 King Street, Circa 1930s.

Buildings on this site have been used as the offices and residences of colonial governors for two hundred years. During most of the nineteenth and early twentieth centuries the building was used as a post office. In 1936-1937 the building was remodeled to resemble a structure in an old painting. The Federal Works Progress Administration (WPA) rebuilt it for use as a post office and customs house. Its weathered wood balconies distinguish the two-story L-shaped building of stucco and coquina with a red tile, pitched roof. Over the years the buildings that have occupied this site have been significantly remodeled, yet with each successive renovation segments of the earlier structures have been successfully incorporated into the new buildings. The last significant reconstruction occurred to accommodate the needs of the postal service. Thankfully, the architect, Mellon C. Greeley, took great pains to preserve aspects of the building's original appearance. His plan, reminiscent of the Spanish styling of the building in 1764, incorporated remnants of three of the old exterior walls, including the north wall, constructed circa 1834; the east wall, built in 1713 and reconstructed in 1786; and almost all of the south wall, constructed in 1713. All of the holdover exterior walls are clearly discernible in Greeley's renovation. ($2-4.)

Government House Museum, 48 King Street, 2008.
The location of the governors' residence on this site reflects a Royal decree that mandated that all Spanish towns have a central plaza for gatherings and processions that was outlined by the community's important buildings, such as the church, market place, and government offices. In this case, the house built for Governor Gonzalo Mendez de Canzo fronted onto the west end of Plaza de la Constitution. In 1964 the federal government transferred the building's title to the State of Florida. Since that year, it has served as the headquarters for the city's historical preservation board, a Visitor Information Center, and a historical museum where visitors could learn about Indian settlements, Ponce de Leon's discovery of Florida, the landing of 1565, battles to expel the French, the Colonial era, the Seminole Indian Wars of the 1800s, and the Henry Flagler era. The Plaza and Government House are beautiful examples of the Old Spanish architecture.

Plaza de la Constitution, 1907.

The Plaza de la Constitution is a landscaped parkway in the center of town between Cathedral and King Streets. It was named to commemorate Spain's adoption of a liberal constitution. At the east end of the Plaza is the Public Market, an open, shed-like structure built in 1824 to replace the original market that dated back to 1598 and was used for public auctioning. Facing the old Public Market is a statue of Juan Ponce de Leon, who is credited with the discovery of Florida. On each side of the Plaza are houses of worship; the Cathedral of St. Augustine, on the north side, was built in 1797 and Trinity Episcopal was the first Episcopal church established in the state after the territory was obtained from Spain in 1821. ($1-3)

Plaza de la Constitution, 2008.

The Plaza is still an open-air town square. It stands at the center of the historic colonial town, one block west of the Bridge of Lions. This view shows the Casa Monica Hotel (Henry Flagler's Cordova Hotel) and the Constitution Monument.

Plaza and Market, 1910.

The City of St. Augustine was founded as a Spanish colony and was laid out in typical Spanish design, with a plaza in the center of town to be used as a park and city center. The park was adorned with shade trees, shrubbery, monuments, sparkling fountains, and an open-air building that housed a public market. In the square stands a monument erected in 1812 in commemoration of the new constitution of Spain and the Spanish provinces; in 1872, a monument honoring Confederate soldiers lost in battle was erected. In the center of this view is the Cathedral of St. Augustine. ($3-5)

Plaza and Market, 2008.

Today the open-air Public Market is dwarfed by large shade trees. A historical marker is located in the center of the photograph. The Constitution and Confederate Monuments are still there.

36

S. A. 113—Ponce de Leon Monument and Circle, St. Augustine, Fla.

Ponce de Leon Circle, 1951.
The magnificent statue of Ponce de Leon, the discoverer of Florida, holds a commanding position in this beautiful circle overlooking the silvery-blue Matanzas Bay. Flowers and trees contributed by the Andrew Anderson and George Gibbs families, two of St. Augustine's more prominent citizens, adorn the circle that surrounds the statue. Note the horse-drawn carriage between the two automobiles. Cancelled 1951, $1-3.

Ponce de Leon Statue, 1940s.
Ponce de Leon has overlooked the ancient city since 1923 when Dr. Andrew Anderson unveiled this statue, a replica of the monument in San Juan, Puerto Rico. Ponce de Leon was governor of the Spanish colony of Puerto Rico before setting out on a voyage in 1513 that resulted in his discovery of Florida.
As for Dr. Anderson (1839-1924), he was a practicing physician, county commissioner, mayor, church trustee, philanthropist, and concerned citizen who was always involved in improving the appearance of the town. ($1-3)

Ponce de Leon Statue, 2008.

Ponce de Leon Circle, 2008.
Some of the colorful flowers are missing in this photograph of the Ponce de Leon Monument and Circle; however, Ponce is still standing in front of the Public Market in the Plaza de la Constitution. The statue and circle are located at the eastern end of the Plaza.

Public Market, East End of Plaza, 1908.
The Public Market was established in the Plaza de la Constitution in 1598 under the supervision of the governor, who set up the first system of weights and measures used in the United States. The present market building, where vegetables and meats were sold during early American times, was rebuilt after the original was destroyed by fire in 1887. ($2-4)

Public Market, 1940s.
Early in the morning farmers from the countryside would display their fruit, vegetables, and meat in wooden stalls under the market roof. Later in the day the market served as the location of an auction or, to the dismay of city fathers, as a hangout for loafers. ($1-3)

Public Market, East End of Plaza, 2008.
The Public Market appears today much the same as it did in the postcard view one hundred years ago. The city park behind the Public Market and extending to the west end of the plaza is also essentially the same now as it was in the postcard view taken in the early twentieth century.

Public Market, 2008.
On market day, the bell in the cupola announced to villagers that produce, fish, and meats were available for sale.

Seawall and South Beach Bridge, St. Augustine, Fla.

South Beach Bridge, 1911.
The wooden bridge to Anastasia Island was a welcome convenience when constructed in 1895. Pedestrians and bicyclists crossed the Matanzas River Bridge for only 5¢. Toll for a double team of horses and wagon with driver was 25¢, with an additional 5-cent charge per person. The St. Johns Electric Company later laid tracks across the bridge, carrying passengers five miles down the island to South Beach, Lighthouse and Alligator Farm. ($8-10)

Station for Anastasia, South, Chautauqua and Crescent Beaches

Bridge of Lions, Looking West, 1930s. ($2-4.)

Bridge of Lions, Looking East, 1940s. ($2-4)

Keepers of the Bridge, 1986.
The marble lions guarding the historic drawbridge in St. Augustine are copies of Roman sculptures made in the 1920s. The originals are in Florence, Italy. The Romanelli Brothers, a sculpturing firm that specializes in making exact replicas of ancient statues, reproduced the St. Augustine lions. ($1-3)

Bridge of Lions, Looking West, 2007.

In 1927 South Beach Bridge was replaced with the Bridge of Lions, a continuation of Cathedral Street across Matanzas River. The bridge featured elements of Mediterranean architecture that was in vogue at the time and thought to reflect Florida's colonial heritage. The bridge drew its name from two marble lions that monitored its western approach. From the beginning people in St. Augustine called the Bridge of Lions the most beautiful bridge in Dixie. It has become a symbol of St. Augustine and is one of the most prominent structures of its skyline. The Florida Department of Transportation is currently doing a $76 million rehabilitation project that will preserve its historic façade and make it stronger. ($1-3)

Bridge of Lions, Looking East, Circa 2006. ($1-3)

Bay Street, North of Plaza, 1920s.
This view of Matanzas Bay shows the Sea Wall, Monson Hotel, Bennett Hotel, and, in the distance, Castillo de San Marcos. Bay Street was renamed Avenida Menendez. ($2-4)

Bennett Hotel, 12 Bay Street, 1930s.
The three-story Bennett Hotel, located on Matanzas Bay, was built on the former site of the Drugless Clinic that Dr. R. C. Conley operated. The Bennett had steam-heated rooms with or without private baths, electric elevators, and a private sunny terrace that overlooked the bay and ocean. James E. Brock was the hotel manager when this postcard was published. The Castillo de San Marcos can be seen in the distance. ($3-5)

Avenida Menendez, North of Plaza, 2008.
In this view is the Hilton St. Augustine Historic Bayfront, Acapulco Mexican Restaurant, and in the distance, part of the old fort. The walkway atop the Sea Wall is on the right.

Acapulco Mexican Restaurant, 12 Avenida Menendez, 2008.
The Acapulco Mexican Restaurant now resides on the site formally occupied by the Bennett Hotel.

Carriage Ride, 1930s.
A carriage ride offered a slow-paced tour along historic downtown streets. Started in 1877, St. Augustine Transfer Company is the oldest continuously operated carriage company in the city. Horse-drawn carriages provided a comfortable, enchanting way to get around. ($2)

Carriage Ride, 2008.
Horse-drawn surreys are reminiscent of St. Augustine's early days as a tourist resort. On narrow twisting side streets, small restaurants offer pilau (a highly seasoned potpourri of rice with boiled meat, fish or fowl), fried shrimp, chowders, and turtle stew. The horse-drawn carriage is still a very popular way to get around in St. Augustine today.

Castillo de San Marcos, 1940s.

The Castillo de San Marcos is the oldest fort in the United States. An attack by the English in 1670 solidified Spanish resolve to better fortify St. Augustine. Groundbreaking for the fort took place in 1672 and the basic structure was completed in 1696. Constructed of massive blocks of coquina stone quarried nearby, the fort was built by Cuban engineers including Ignacio Daza. Skilled stone masons from Havana, slaves, and Indians participated in its construction. With its twelve-foot thick walls, encircling moat, dependable water supply, and latrine flushed by tidal action, all 1,500 residents of St. Augustine found refuge here in times of trouble. The coquina structure measures 324 by 311 feet. There are twenty-nine casemates along with two end rooms within the Castillo, with cannons commanding the harbor entrance. ($2-4)

Castillo de San Marcos, 2008.

The Spanish flag still flies in this view of the old fort. A diamond-shaped bastion protects each corner of the Castillo. From the bastion the adjacent walls could be protected from an attacking force, and in conjunction with the neighboring bastions, a deadly cross fire could be turned on any force that got too close. The bastions provided the cross fire necessary to protect the main walls.

Castillo de San Marcos, Main Entrance, 1909.

The Castillo de San Marcos was built to protect the Spanish settlements and Spanish Treasure fleets. The Castillo survived two major sieges and was never captured by an enemy during battle. The fort has walls twenty-one feet high, a moat that surrounded it, bastions on the corners, heavy casemates, dungeons, and subterranean passages. The Castillo took twenty-three years to build and cost more than 138,000 pesos ($218,360). The design of the fort is "stellar." It has a square central courtyard with a series of storage rooms around it and diamond-shaped bastions at each corner. Cancelled 1909, $3-5.

Castillo de San Marcos, Main Entrance, 2008.

Not much has changed to this entranceway of the fort. The moat was dry and used to keep livestock during times of attack. This dry moat served as a major obstacle to infantry attacking the Castillo. The National Park Service had water in the moat from 1938-1996. The water was removed to insure the structural integrity of the fort. The moat and towers helped the fort withstand many assaults.

Castillo de San Marcos, Ramp, 1907.
Spanish soldiers moved quickly up the ramp to the "fighting deck" on top of the fort. The steps were added in modern times for visitor safety. The supporting arch, while unusual in this country, is typical of Spanish military architecture in the 1700s. ($3-5)

Castillo de San Marcos, Ramp, 2008.
The angled stairway led to the fort's "gun deck." The fort could accommodate a garrison of 1,000 men and one hundred guns.

Castillo de San Marcos, Courtyard, 1910s.
Beautifully arched casemates and interesting cornices testify to the workmanship and imagination of the Spanish builders. The fort contains guardrooms, dungeons, living quarters for the garrison, storerooms, and a chapel. Nearly all the rooms open on a court about a hundred feet square. ($1-3)

Castillo de San Marlos, Courtyard, 2008.
In this present-day view, the courtyard now has grass in its center. The entrance to the chapel is on the left. From the fort's watchtower (on the top right) the sentries kept watch over the inlet and sea.

CHIEF OSCEOLA OF THE SEMINOLES CONFINED IN COURT ROOM.

FORT MARION, ST. AUGUSTINE, FLA.

Castillo de San Marcos, Osceola's Cell, 1920s.
An important service of the fort was as a military prison. Those imprisoned were Seminoles in 1837-38, Plains Indians in 1875-78, Apaches in 1886-87, and Army deserters during the Spanish-American War. In October 1837, almost a hundred of Florida's Seminole Indians were captured under a white flag of truce just south of St. Augustine. Included in the group were the famous warriors Osceola and Caocoochee. Most of these prisoners spent six weeks locked up at the fort. Twenty of the prisoners, among them Caocoochee, staged an escape on the night of November 29, 1837. Soon after, Osceola was moved to Fort Moultrie in Charleston, South Carolina where he died on January 30, 1838. Use of the fort ended in 1900, when the Army withdrew its troops from St. Augustine. ($2-4)

Castillo de San Marcos, Osceola's Cell, 2008.
The cell that imprisoned Seminole leader Osceola is now missing a door and its famous guest.

46

Castillo de San Marcos, Hot Shot Oven, 1910.
A view of the hot shot oven and watchtower; in this oven shots (cannon balls) were heated to fire at wooden vessels. At the rear may be bullet holes in the wall where prisoners were executed. ($1-3)

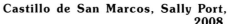

Castillo de San Marcos, Sally Port, circa 1910.
The Sally Port is the only entrance and exit of the Castillo. Directly off the Sally Port are the Spanish guardrooms and the prison. The drawbridge was the primary way of securing the Castillo. By using the cranks located beneath the trapdoors and the counterweights, the drawbridge could be raised and lowered in fifteen minutes by three men. ($1-3)

Castillo de San Marcos, Sally Port, 2008.
This is still the only entrance to the old fort. A National Park Service employee stands by to answer any questions that visitors may have.

Castillo de San Marcos, Hot Shot Oven, 2008.
View of the hot shot oven and watchtower; the sentry box or watchtower at the corner of the fort provided shelter for men on watch during bad weather. The sentry on duty would give the alarm when an enemy was sighted.

Castle Warden, 19 San Marco Avenue, 1940s.

This Moorish Revival castle, the largest poured concrete residence in the city, was built in 1887 as the winter residence of William G. Warden, a partner in the Standard Oil Company. The 23-room house remained in the Warden family through the 1930s. In 1941 Norton Baskin and his wife, Marjorie Kinnan Rawlings, remodeled the structure and maintained the castle as the Castle Warden Hotel until 1946. Marjorie Rawlings, known for her authorship of *The Yearling, Cross Creek* and *South Moon Under,* divided her time between St. Augustine and her house in Cross Creek in central Florida. Baskin sold the property in 1946 and, after changing hands several times, the castle structure became the now famous Ripley's Believe It or Not! Museum in 1950. ($3-5)

Ripley's Believe It Or Not! Museum, 19 San Marco Avenue, 2008.

Ripley's Believe It Or Not! of St. Augustine is the original "Believe It Or Not! Odditorium" in the Ripley Entertainment family consisting of sixty-three attractions in eleven countries. More than 13 million people visit a Ripley's attraction each year. St. Augustine's Ripley's features more than 750 exhibits to fascinate, delight, and entertain people of all ages. You will find a gigantic Ferris wheel, the world's largest moving erector model containing 19,507 pieces standing 21.3 feet tall. See Beauregard, a six-legged cow that lived fourteen years with two extra legs growing from its back. Robert Ripley's life was an unbelievable adventure. For more than forty years, he explored the uncanny and witnessed the amazing. During his career, he visited 198 countries, collecting oddities that would later create the fabulous world of Ripley's Believe It Or Not!

Cathedral of St. Augustine, 38 Cathedral Place, 1952.

A major landmark in St. Augustine is the Cathedral of St. Augustine. Founded in 1793 as a little parish church, it was completed in 1797. Building material was coquina stone quarried on Anastasia Island. The original was 120 x 42 feet, typical of many churches built by the Spanish during the eighteenth century. The King's engineer, Mariano de la Rogue, created the ornamental molding recesses and cornices to relieve the starkness of the façade. Doric columns on either side of the rounded arch doorway supported the entablature. In 1870, the Diocese of St. Augustine was formed and the small church became a Cathedral. The Great Fire of 1887 destroyed everything except the Cathedral walls. A belltower and transepts were added after the fire; the belltower was made from cast-in-place concrete. The wooden roof was replaced with tiles. Cancelled 1952, $1-3.

Basilica-Cathedral of St. Augustine, 38 Cathedral Place, 2008.

The Cathedral of St. Augustine was designated a Minor Basilica in September of 1977, and the Basilica-Cathedral was designated a National Historic Landmark by the U.S. Department of the Interior. The Basilica-Cathedral of St. Augustine has the oldest written parish records in the nation, dating from 1594, and is one of the oldest Catholic religious buildings in the United States. The Cathedral is located across from the Plaza in downtown St. Augustine. The interior represents Spanish heritage embellished by ornate décor. Twelve large stained glass windows depict events in the life of St. Augustine of Hippo. Another large window, to the right of the front door, honors St. Cecelia, patron of music. The windows were made in Germany and installed in 1909. The fourteen oil paintings of the Stations of the Cross are copies of those in the Pauline Chapel of the Vatican. Each crossbeam bears the coat of arms of a bishop of St. Augustine, beginning with Bishop Verot, 1870-1876. The floor is Cuban tile, made of cement. The murals throughout the Cathedral are by Hugo Ohlms, a local artist.

Cathedral Street Looking West, 1910.
On the left is the Public Market in the Plaza de la Constitución. In the middle of this view is the Cathedral of St. Augustine. ($3-5)

Cathedral Street Looking West, 2008.
This view shows the Basilica-Cathedral of St. Augustine and the tallest structure in the city, which houses a bank. Local architect Francis Hollingsworth, who was known for his Mediterranean Revival style, designed the bank building, which was built in 1926.

CHARLOTTE STREET.

Charlotte Street, 1915.
Like all Spanish towns in this hemisphere, St. Augustine was laid out on a specific grid pattern prescribed by royal ordinance. Street widths were between twelve and twenty-two feet and the crossing lanes eight feet wide. The narrow street plan has not changed much since it was laid out in 1572. In 1867 Charlotte Street, not St. George Street, was St. Augustine's main commercial street. It was first known as La Calle de Los Mercados, the street of the merchants. It was also known as the "street that lead to the barracks." ($3-5)

Charlotte Street, 2008.
Fires have destroyed many of the aged buildings on Charlotte Street but it retains much of its old time characteristics in sections. Many of the current structures have balconies that reflect architectural charm. This street is today a National Historic Landmark.

City Gate, Looking South, 1902.
The City Gate, located on St. George Street at Orange Street, consists of two square coquina pylons with concave peaks capped with representations of the Moorish pomegranate. The gate was attached to sections of an old coquina wall and a moat, and was part of the city defense system. Construction of the original coquina gate, replacing earlier wooden ones, began in 1745, but the present more ornamental structures were erected in 1804, and for many years guarded the drawbridge over a moat. ($3-5)

City Gate, Looking South, 2008.
St. George Street is St. Augustine's main pedestrian thoroughfare. During the First Spanish Period (1513-1763), it was known as the "Street of the Governor." In 1763, the British named it in honor of King George III.

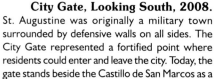

circa 1880 *The City Gate* *St. Augustine, Florida*

City Gate, Looking South, 1880s.
During the days of Spanish occupation, St. Augustine's inner line of defense consisted of a wall extending from the Castillo de San Marcos to San Sebastian River. As the town was surrounded on three sides by water, the gate offered, at that time, the only entrance to the city and once had heavy doors to seal off the town at night. Circa 1945, $1-3.

City Gate, Looking South, 2008.
St. Augustine was originally a military town surrounded by defensive walls on all sides. The City Gate represented a fortified point where residents could enter and leave the city. Today, the gate stands beside the Castillo de San Marcos as a reminder of the Spanish heritage of St. Augustine and is now a part of Castillo de San Marcos National Monument.

Civic Center, San Marco Avenue, 1941.

The St. Augustine Civic Center was one of few major buildings in the city constructed during the Depression era of the 1930s, built in 1937 on the former site of the San Marco Hotel under the auspices of the Federal Works Progress Administration (WPA), an agency organized to alleviate unemployment. St. Augustine architect Fred A. Henderich designed the building, which was constructed of coquina, the most historically significant building material used in St. Augustine. This $68,000 Civic Center had an auditorium seating capacity of nine hundred, club rooms for tourists, and broad porches overlooking Castillo de San Marcos and the Atlantic Ocean. The grounds were well equipped with shuffleboard, tennis and roque courts, and baseball and football fields. Cancelled 1941, $1-3.

Visitor Information Center, San Marco Avenue, 2008.

The St. Augustine Civic Center served as a community center until the 1950s, when the Chamber of Commerce renamed it the Visitor Information Center and began using it for tourist orientation. Its location, north of the old city, is where most travelers arrive and where sufficient parking is available. After parking their cars in adjacent lots, visitors today can obtain information about the city in the information center, walk to the Castillo de San Marcos, which is the major regional tourist attraction, pass through the City Gate, and walk down St. George Street to the Plaza de la Constitution. Visitors can also ride trolleys from the information center to view historic sites. Over a million people annually visit St. Augustine. In 1991, the City of St. Augustine assumed responsibility for management of the building and its information services function.

Courthouse, Treasury and Charlotte Streets, 1918.

In 1907, St. Johns County moved into a new $55,000 courthouse, a Spanish-style building with a wide hall extending the length of the courthouse. Destroyed in the 1914 fire, the brick building was replaced by the structure shown in 1918. The St. Johns County Courthouse was later relocated o the remodeled Cordova Hotel (Alcazar Annex). ($15-17)

Courthouse Site, Treasury and Charlotte Streets, 2008.

The Courthouse was razed and the site is now a parking lot for offices in the bank building.

Dodge's Curiosity Shop, 54 St. George Street, 1920s.

This two-story coquina block building covered with rusty stucco, and three dormer windows and a tall coquina chimney, was occupied by a curio, souvenir, and antique shop. The house, also known as the Paredes House, was claimed to be the oldest house in St. Augustine. However, it was later determined to have been built between 1805 and 1813 by Juan Paredes, a mariner from Mallorca. It was known as Dodge's Old Curiosity Shop when this postcard photo was taken. ($3-5)

OLD CURIOSITY SHOP, ST. GEORGE STREET.

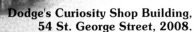

Dodge's Curiosity Shop Building, 54 St. George Street, 2008.

The home of John Paredes, a two-story coquina block building with rusty stucco, three dormer windows and a tall coquina chimney, was later occupied by a curio, souvenir, and antique shop. Also owned at one time by the St. Augustine Historical Society, today it's the home of the St. Augustine Art Glass Craft Gallery, a shop that sells all type of glass items. The house was restored during the 1970s.

Dr. Peck House, 143 St. George Street, 1990s. The stonewalls of the Dr. Peck House date from before 1750 and were part of a house owned by the Royal Treasurer in the First Spanish Period (1513-1763). During the British Period (1763-1783), it served for a time as the home of Governor John Moultrie. In 1837 Dr. Seth S. Peck purchased the house and rebuilt it, using the old walls and adding the frame second story. It remained in the Peck family until willed to the City of St. Augustine in 1931. A generous grant from the Flagler Foundation permitted extensive restoration in 1968. ($1-3)

Dr. Peck House, 143 St. George Street, 2008. The Dr. Peck House, also called the Peck-Peck House, is owned by the City of St. Augustine and operated and maintained by the Women's Exchange. The house has a gift shop and daily tours are available to view the period furnishings and artwork. Recognized for more than a century as one of the city's finest houses, many of its extraordinary furnishings have, for the most part, been a part of its décor for over 150 years. The St. George Street pedestrian mall ends one block south of this building.

"THE DRUGLESS CLINIC" ON THE BAY FRONT,
ST. AUGUSTINE, FLORIDA

Drugless Clinic, 12 Bay Street, 1930s.
Dr. R. C. Conley operated this clinic, almost directly opposite the Castillo de San Marcos. The clinic was equipped to diagnose and treat 98 percent of all human ailments and was one of the finest and most modern in the south. The clinic specialized in the diagnosis and treatment of difficult cases. The site of this clinic later became the Bennett Hotel and is currently occupied by the Acapulco Mexican Restaurant. Cancelled 1942, $3-5.

Acapulco Mexican Restaurant, 12 Avenida Menendez, 2008.
The Acapulco Mexican Restaurant now occupies the site of the former Drugless Clinic. Across from this restaurant is where the horse-drawn carriages park along Avenida Menendez. Visitors eating at the restaurant also have an excellent view of the Castillo de San Marcos.

Florida House Hotel, Treasury and St. George Streets, 1910.
The four-story Florida House Hotel opened in 1835 and featured gas lighting and a steam elevator for guests. At the time St. Augustine had about three hundred accommodations for tourists. It was destroyed by fire on April 2, 1914, possibly by rats chewing on matches. ($8-10)

The House of Ireland, Treasury and St. George Streets, 2008.
A gift shop of Irish items (shown) and other adjoining businesses now occupy the site of the old Florida House Hotel.

Florida School for the Deaf, 207 San Marco Avenue, 1898.
The Florida School for the Deaf was founded in 1885 by Thomas Hines Coleman, himself a deaf mute. The school originally consisted of four rambling wooden structures. The central building was the residence of the superintendent and teachers. On each side of the central building was a two-story building measuring 35 by 60 feet. The lower stories of these buildings were study rooms while the upper rooms were used for sleeping quarters for the students. Behind the superintendent's residence was the dining room in a one-story, 25 by 40-foot building. ($5-7)

Florida School for the Deaf and Blind, 207 San Marco Avenue, 2008.
In place of the original buildings, there are now several handsome buildings of brick and hollow tile. The school occupies several acres and is laid out to meet the needs of the students and every effort is made to provide curricula that will help them find their place in life. In spite of physical handicaps, the students are enthusiastic athletes; the school has a basketball, baseball, and football team that compete regularly with other teams in the state. This school is one of the oldest educational institutions in the state. Such notable musical contemporaries as Ray Charles and Stevie Wonder attended it.

Fountain of Youth Park, San Marco Avenue Entrance, 1930s.
The popular Fountain of Youth Park is located about six blocks north of the Castillo de San Marcos. Entrance to the park is located on Myrtle Street off San Marco Avenue. Important archaeological discoveries at the park include the first Christian Indian burials in North America with Mission Period interments; Timucua Indian hut foundations and relics; artifacts indicating Timucua Indian habitation for more than 1,000-years prior to Ponce de Leon's arrival; and evidence that Pedro Menendez' colony occupied the site during the sixteenth century. The park has a prehistoric Indian spring that still flows. ($1-3)

Fountain of Youth National Archaeological Park, San Marco Avenue Entrance, 2008.
The archaeological park contains foundations and artifacts of the first St. Augustine mission and colony.

Fountain of Youth Statue of Ponce de Leon, 11 Magnolia Avenue, Circa 1950.
Statue of Juan Ponce de Leon in the Fountain of Youth Park—the statue was dedicated in a program broadcast by the U.S. Department of State on the 437th anniversary of Ponce's landing. ($3-5)

Fountain of Youth Statue of Ponce de Leon, 2008.

Fountain of Youth, Indian Burial Ground, 2008.
The exposed skeletons were reburied at a Catholic consecration ceremony in 1991. Today there is a large photograph of the exposed skeletons in the protective Indian Burial Ground Building.

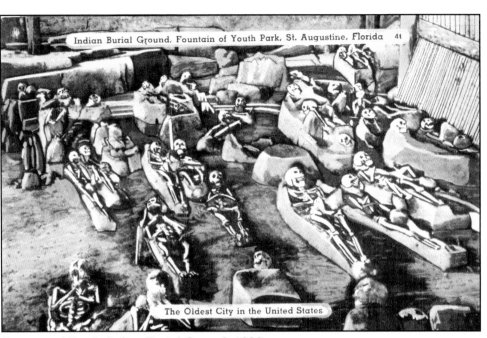

Indian Burial Ground, Fountain of Youth Park, St. Augustine, Florida 41

The Oldest City in the United States

Fountain of Youth, Indian Burial Ground, 1930s.
Protected by a massive reproduction of a Timucua Indian communal house, many Indian burials were excavated by Dr. M. W. Stirling of the Smithsonian Institute and give evidence of the once flowering culture existing before the arrival of Ponce de Leon in 1513. Now covered with soil, for many years over one hundred skeletons were exposed in the exact position as they were found. ($2-4)

Fountain of Youth, Well, 1930s.
The Fountain of Youth Spring is one of the focal points of the Fountain of Youth, preserved as a memorial to the Spanish explorer who pioneered the bringing of European civilization to the shores of the United States. The Fountain of Youth spring water was advertised as preserving youth for all that drank the water. ($1-3)

Fountain of Youth, Spring House, 1910.
The Spring Well is located in this Spring House. Ancient artifacts and lush vegetation decorate the grounds of the Fountain of Youth. ($1-3)

Fountain of Youth, Well, 2008.

Fountain of Youth, Spring House, 2008.
Two archways of the Spring House have been closed and climbing vines cover the entire building.

Golf Course, 1902.
The ladies in this view are playing golf on grounds surrounding the historic fort. The nine-hole St. Augustine Golf Club stretched between Riberia Street and the bay, and included much of the fort green. Local players and hotel guests used the course from the latter 1800s until well into the twentieth century. This was the first golf course in Florida in 1895. ($10-12)

Golf Course Site, 2008.
The golfers are gone in this current view of the fort lawn.

Magnolia Hotel, Hypolita and St. George Streets, 1907.

The seventeen-room Magnolia Hotel, located near the southwest corner of St. George and Hypolita Streets, opened in 1847. The hotel, owned by Burroughs E. Carr, was considered to be the finest rooming establishment in the city when it opened. By 1853 the hotel was enlarged to forty-five rooms. In the 1880s the Magnolia was remodeled as a 250-room, three-story hotel and became one of the oldest and most popular tourist accommodations in the city. The hotel burned down on December 27, 1926. It was the last of the massive wooden structures that predated the Flagler hotels. ($8-10)

Spanish Plaza, Hypolita and St. George Streets, 2008.
A collection of shops along St. George Street now occupy the site of the old Magnolia Hotel.

Mission of Nombre De Dios, 27 Ocean Avenue, 1915.

The Mission of Nombre de Dios and Lady of La Leche Shrine are on the site of the 1565 landing of Pedro Menendez and where the first Catholic Mass was said. Menendez planted the Cross, Father Francisco Lopez de Mendoza Grajales offered the Mass, and our American life began. This all took place fifty-five years before the pilgrims landed at Plymouth Rock. English soldiers stationed in Georgia abandoned the Shrine during border raids. It was rebuilt by Bishop Verot in 1873 and blown down by a storm a year later. Bishop Curley erected it in 1918. In 1925 Mrs. Hardin restored and furnished it as a Chapel, in memory of General Martin D. Hardin. ($1-3)

Mission of Nombre De Dios, 27 Ocean Avenue, 2008.

The Mission of Nombre de Dios includes a small chapel and cemetery. The La Leche Chapel is a late-1700s reconstruction of the original building, and, in the subsequent two centuries and more, has itself been repaired several times following damage inflected by hurricanes.

Monson House Hotel, 32 Bay Street, 1906.
Beautiful private homes faced the bay front and flanked either side of the Monson House Hotel, a popular St. Augustine accommodation in the early twentieth century. It was owned by A. V. Monson and could accommodate three hundred guests. It was destroyed in an April 2, 1914 fire and replaced in the 1920s by the Monson Hotel. ($10-12)

Monson Hotel, 32 Bay Street, 1928.
In 1926, the Monson Hotel replaced the Monson House Hotel, which was destroyed by fire in 1914. The following advertisement came from a 1928 edition of *Foster's Florida Standard Guide*: "Offering the personality and atmosphere of a refined home, with the added convenience of a first-class hotel—one hundred cheerful rooms and sixty private baths." The Monson Hotel was razed in the 1960s and replaced with the Monson Motor Lodge, a key site during the 1964 civil rights rallies and demonstrations. Dr. Martin Luther King, Jr. was arrested at the lodge during a sit-in and African-American protestors had muriatic acid poured into the water when they refused to get out of the motel's "whites only" swimming pool. The motel was razed in 2002. ($4-6)

Hilton St. Augustine Historic Bayfront, 32 Avenida Menendez, 2008.
A Hilton hotel was built on the site of the former Monson Hotel and Monson Motor Lodge in 2005. This bay front hotel has seventy-two rooms in nineteen buildings designed by architect Gerald Dixon. The buildings were designed to fit in with the old architecture of surrounding buildings. The southernmost building of the Hilton is strikingly similar to the old Vedder House that occupied the site prior to the first Monson lodging.

Oldest Schoolhouse, 14 St. George Street, 1920s.
Originally a small homestead, America's oldest wooden schoolhouse first appeared on St. Augustine's tax rolls in 1716. The schoolmaster lived upstairs with his family and used the ground floor as a classroom. Boys and girls were taught in the same classroom, making the St. Augustine school the first in the nation to go co-ed. Located near the City Gate, the Oldest Schoolhouse is a surviving expression of another time. Built over two hundred years ago while Florida was under the rule of Spain, it was constructed of red cedar and cypress and put together with wooden pegs and handmade nails. ($1-3)

Oldest Schoolhouse, Back View, 1930s.
The Oldest Schoolhouse, a vine-clad clapboard structure of hand-hewn red cedar planks with a coquina chimney and a dormer window, was a residence in the eighteenth century. It was used for a schoolhouse before the Civil War. ($1-3)

Oldest Schoolhouse, Back View, 2008.
The courtyard of the old schoolhouse is now set up for school children who visit the historic site regularly on field trips.

Oldest Schoolhouse, 14 St. George Street, 2008.
The Oldest Schoolhouse requires constant repair work to keep it in shape for visitors.

Oldest Schoolhouse, Classroom, 1930s.
The schoolmaster and his wife lived upstairs, above the small (and oldest) classroom. Their kitchen was separated from the main building because of the threat of fire and to spare the house of any excess heat during the long summers. ($2-4)

Oldest Schoolhouse, Classroom, 2008.
Today, visitors can sit with the schoolmaster and his pupils as they re-create what school life was like. Visitors can compare their school days with those of the Old Days!

Old Jail, St. Augustine, Florida

Old Jail, 167 San Marco Avenue, 1890s.
The Old Jail, completed in 1891 and built with funds provided by railroad magnate Henry M. Flagler, housed prisoners for over sixty years. It's one of the surviving nineteenth century jails. Here, Sheriff Joe Perry and his wife, Lou, lived and worked for $2 a day. The building held seventy-two prisoners and served the county until 1953. The massive Queen Anne style stucco-on-brick building was placed on the National Registry of Historic Places in 1987. Circa 1930s, $3-5

Old Jail, 167 San Marco Avenue, 2008.
Visitors to the Old Jail can imagine themselves being processed as an inmate in 1908. The Old Jail is one of the very few surviving nineteenth century incarceration facilities in the state and is the oldest government building in St. Johns County. Visitors learn about justice and punishment when Florida was America's southernmost frontier.

Ribera House, 26 St. George Street, 1965.
When the Spanish left St. Augustine in 1763, Juan Ribera occupied a house at 26 St. George Street that had been built around 1750. Thereafter, it became vacant, fell into decay, and in 1770 was sold for its stone. During the British Period (1763-1783), a wooden house was built on the foundation of the earlier structure. This house, in turn, was destroyed. In 1965, Juan Ribera's house was reconstructed on the original foundation to illustrate the pure Spanish architecture of the period. Behind the plain wall blossomed a stunning Spanish garden. ($2-4)

Ribera House, 26 St. George Street, 2008.
This is typical of a "fine" house, occupied by a prominent well-to-do family. Unlike most two-story houses in this historic section of St. Augustine, it had two stories from the beginning, whereas most were one-story flattops upon which a wooden second level was added during the English occupation (1763-1783). Like all First Spanish Period (1513-1763) homes it had no glass in the windows, only shutters. Entrance from the street through a gateway into the patio is typical. Today the reconstructed Ribera House serves as an orientation center for the San Agustin Antiguo living history museum just across St. George Street.

Public Burial Ground, Orange Street and San Marco Avenue, 1898.
When Florida became a possession of the United States in 1821, there developed a need for a Protestant cemetery. The City of St. Augustine gained access to a half-acre plot to serve as a resting place for non-Catholics. The public burying ground, sometimes called the Huguenot Cemetery, was the area's first public cemetery. A yellow fever epidemic swept over the populace soon after, and the cemetery was put to good use. Many Protestant pioneers to the Florida Territory are buried here. Often such burials, made at public expense, went unmarked. The cemetery is surrounded by a coquina wall and is overgrown with moss-hung cedars and magnolias. ($5-7)

Public Burial Ground, Orange Street and San Marco Avenue, 2008.
The Presbyterian Church acquired the cemetery in 1832 and continues to own it. From then until 1884, when interments were discontinued, this was St. Augustine's principal non-Catholic cemetery. The name "Huguenot" was attached to the cemetery later in the nineteenth century. The cemetery is closed to the public; however, it can be viewed outside the fenced area along Orange Street or from the sidewalk on San Marco Avenue.

Bay Street, St. Augustine, Fla.

Sea Wall Along Bay Street, Circa 1910.

This view of the Sea Wall shows Bay Street and the Castillo de San Marcos in the background. The Spanish began construction of the wall shortly after 1690, but the English completed it in the 1770s. Between 1835 and 1842 the United States Government built a new wall of coquina rock with a heavy granite coping. The Sea Wall extends from the north boundary of the Castillo de San Marcos to a point opposite St. Francis Barracks. It was built as a necessary protection against encroachment of Matanza Bay's waters. A walk along the wall was a pleasant diversion in the 1880s. Capo's Bath House, shown on the right, was a bayfront recreation facility built in 1870 for timid swimmers to paddle about in indoor comfort. The bathhouse was a circular stone and wooden structure in the bay, where men and women could enjoy hot, cold, seawater, and sulphur baths at high tide. The popular bathing spot burned in 1914. ($8-10)

Sea Wall Along Avenida Menendez, 2008.

Part of the old Spanish wall is, today, beneath Bay Street (now Avenida Menendez). The Sea Wall is still a beautiful walk for tourists. In this view the Acapulco Mexican Restaurant is on the far left and the Castillo de San Marcos is on the right.

San Marco Hotel, San Marco Avenue, 1896.
One of the most striking sights to greet visitors to nineteenth century St. Augustine were the sixty-foot spires of the elegant San Marco Hotel that towered beyond the City Gate. The San Marco was located on a fifteen-acre site, one of the high spots in the ancient city, that overlooked the Castillo de San Marcos, Matanzas Bay, and as far as the eye can see, the beautiful Atlantic Ocean. Henry M. Flagler and his wife stayed there shortly after it opened in 1886. The six-story wooden luxury hotel rivaled even Flagler's grand creations. But the future of the sprawling Victorian hotel was not destined to be as bright and lasting as the facilities erected by Flagler. In 1897 fire erupted and destroyed the hotel. ($5-7)

Visitor Information Center, 2008.
In 1937, with assistance from the Federal Works Progress Administration, the Civic Center was built on the site of the San Marco Hotel. In the 1950s the Chamber of Commerce renamed it the Visitor Information Center and began using it for visitor information. The structure, built by architect Fred A. Hendricht, features a stucco finish with coquina shells.

Spanish Treasury, 143 St. George Street, 1930.

A two-story, flat-roofed, white-shuttered house, the first story of yellow stucco stone, the second of wood, was built in 1690. This was the residence of the Royal Treasurer, Juan Esteban de Pena, toward the end of the First Spanish Period (1513-1763). As he handled the royal funds that the city depended on for support, he was quite an important person. Under British rule, it became the home of Lieutenant Governor John Moultrie and an east wing was added. In 1784 Governor Patrick Tonyn moved in. It was vacant for part of the Second Spanish Period (1783-1821), but then became a home for slaves. Dr. Seth Peck of New York bought it in 1837 and added a wooden second floor. ($1-3)

The Old Spanish Treasury, St. Augustine, Fla.   34

The Oldest City in the United States   60736

Dr. Peck House, 143 St. George Street, 2008.

Dr. John Peck's house and gardens remains one of St. Augustine's most interesting houses. Dr. Peck's granddaughter, Anna Burt, willed the home to the city and the Woman's Exchange took over its maintenance. Opened as a museum in 1932, it contains a rare collection of old furniture, glass, china, and paintings—possessions of the Peck-Burt family, who owned the property for a hundred years starting in 1830. There is also an interesting and valuable collection of Spanish relics. In the garden there is an abundance of rare and beautiful plants and part of the ancient coquina wall still stands. The house is also called the Peck-Peck House.

ST. GEORGE STREET, ST. AUGUSTINE, FLA.

St. George Street, 1902.
St. Augustine is a charming city with both "old world" and "early Southern" atmosphere because of the many buildings that have been carefully and lovingly restored. Typical of city streets in St. Augustine is St. George Street. The "old world" feeling is enhanced by many of the structures along this street, some with balconies, reflecting architectural charm. A walk on St. George Street is a wonderful way to experience the mixture of old and new in St. Augustine. ($15-17)

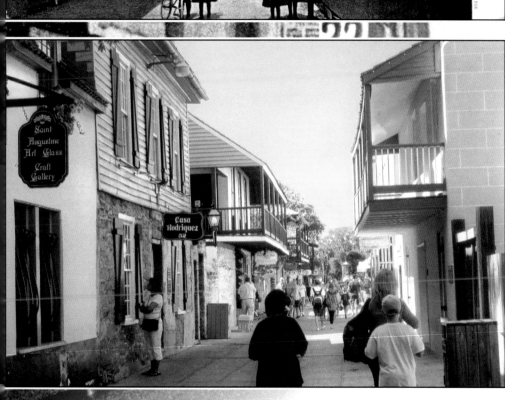

St. George Street, 2008.
Today St. George Street is a pedestrian thoroughfare. In the nineteenth century it was a busy city street. It's interesting to note that Presidents of the United States, captured Indian chiefs, famous villains and pirates, and millions of tourists have walked down this street. Most tourists walk down St. George Street without knowing much about it. For a long time it was known as "the street of San Patricio." The English renamed it George Street in honor of King George III. When the Spanish returned in 1783, the street was renamed Calle Jorge and around 1793 it was called St. George Street in honor of the dragon-killing Saint. The name has stuck for the past two hundred years. Since the 1960s, the city has reserved St. George Street for pedestrians, allowing tourists to walk easily from the Castillo de San Marcos to the central Plaza.

St. George Street, St. Augustine, Fla.

St. George Street Looking North, 1916.

St. George Street has always been one of the most interesting streets in St Augustine. Reconstruction began in this area in the 1960s and continues to go on throughout the city. Cancelled 1916, $10-12.

St. George Street Looking North, 1987.

St. Augustine is a city with an European atmosphere. When visitors cross the little bridge over San Sebastian River they feel as if they have left America behind and entered an European city. The traffic slows to a crawl, but no one seems to mind. There are as many people as there are cars using the narrow streets. More than any other city in the nation, St. Augustine is a city for people, built low to the ground and concentrated within a small area. It has not expanded its corporate limits since the 1930s, and consequently, the explosive growth of other parts of the state has not affected St Augustine. A thirty-five-foot height limit on buildings and other strict regulations set by the Historic Architectural Review Board, the watchdog agency for urban development, not only protect the city's appearance but also give visitors the illusion that they are walking in a medieval walled city, although there are no walls.

NARROWEST IN U. S. 6 FEET 1 INCH. TREASURY STREET

ST. AUGUSTINE, Fla. Treasury Street, the Narrowest Street in the U. S.

Treasury Street, Looking West from Bay Street, 1909.
Up this tunnel-like street, the narrowest in St. Augustine, pirates once stormed toward the house of the Spanish Treasurer, located at the intersection of Treasury and St. George streets. The narrow street barely reaches a seven-foot width in some sections. The name derives from the fact that the King's treasury faced on one of its corners. The Vedder House was located on the north side of this street. Cancelled 1909, $3-5.

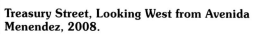

Treasury Street, Looking West from Avenida Menendez, 2008.
Tourists enjoy walking down the narrowest street in the city. The Vedder House was located on the north side of the street and later became part of the Monson Hotel. That site is now occupied by one of the nineteen buildings of the Hilton St. Augustine Historic Bayfront. Wachovia Bank occupies the southern corner of Treasury Street and Avenida Menendez.

Old Vedder House on the Bay,
Corner Treasury Street, Oldest in U. S.

Copyright-12-Harris Co.

Vedder House, 42 Bay Street, 1910s.

Lieutenant Antonio Rodrigues Afrian owned the Vedder House in 1763. The two-story coquina structure was the residence of John Leslie of the trading firm Panton and Leslie, which operated during the British Period (1763-1783) and Second Spanish Period (1783-1821). The house was later occupied by Nicolas Vedder. In 1899 the house was purchased by the St. Augustine Historical Society and used as the Vedder Museum where Vedder's collection of ancient maps and relics were put on display. The structure and its contents were destroyed in a 1914 fire. One of the remaining walls was incorporated into the Monson House Hotel. ($8-10)

Vedder House Site, 42 Avenida Menendez, 2008.

The site of the former Vedder House is now occupied by the southernmost building of the Hilton St. Augustine Historic Bayfront.

Chapter Six:
South of the Plaza

Aviles Street. Old Spanish Quarter

Aviles Street, 1920s.
Picturesque old Aviles Street was named after Pedro Menendez de Aviles, the city's founder. Aviles Street is the shortest and one of the oldest streets in the ancient city. Starting at the town Plaza and King Street, it runs south to Bridge Street and ends there. Originally called Hospital Street, it is only .2 of a mile long. During the 1930s the art colony along the street displayed their products on gray coquina garden walls and the artists often worked at easels beneath fig trees in open courtyards. Many of the gardens, secluded behind high walls, were laid out a century ago; their patios were sheltered by pomegranate, fig, and sweet orange trees, fruits brought over at an early date by the Spaniards. ($1-3)

Aviles Street, 2008.
Quaint narrow Aviles Street reflects St. Augustine's Spanish colonial origin. This street, located in the old section of the city, contains several restored historical buildings, shops, restaurants, and art galleries. The Gaspar Papy House, O'Reilly House, Spanish Military Hospital, and Ximenez-Fatio House are located on this narrow street.

CASA MONICA HOTEL IN THE 1890'S

Cordova Hotel, 95 Cordova Street, 1902.

Franklin W. Smith, Henry Flagler's rival in St. Augustine, built the Spanish-Moorish style Casa Monica Hotel in 1888, as indicated on this postcard view. Flagler later bought the hotel, renamed it the Cordova, and made it thrive by marketing his three St. Augustine hotels together. The Cordova became the social resort, a whirl of balls, parties, and fairs. Teachers were even hired to tutor the children of the wealthy. Ward Foster's bookstore occupied the corner shop in the Cordova Hotel. In 1902, a bridge was built from the second story of the Cordova, connecting it to the Alcazar Hotel. The Cordova's name was again changed a year later to Alcazar's Annex. The economic pressures of the Great Depression forced the closing of the hotel in 1932. In 1962, St. Johns County acquired the Annex for use as its courthouse. ($10-12)

Casa Monica Hotel, 95 Cordova Street, 2008.

The Casa Monica Hotel, originally built in 1888 by Franklin W. Smith, was purchased and operated by Henry Flagler. It thrived as the Cordova Hotel from 1888 to 1902, but lost much of its luster during the late 1920s and eventually closed during the Great Depression. In the mid-1990s, Orlando developer Richard Kessler purchased the courthouse and transformed it back into a glorious hotel reminiscent of its heyday during the gilded Age. It opened as the Casa Monica Hotel for the second time in December 1999. The modern Casa Monica Hotel has a Moorish-Revival design, resembling a medieval European castle. Five towers distinguish the property, including a corner tower seven stories high. The new Casa Monica has 137 rooms, a grand lobby, a fine-dining restaurant, and two grand staircases.

FLAGLER HOSPITAL, ST. AUGUSTINE, FLA.

Flagler Hospital, Marine Street, 1921. The elegant three-story brick and concrete Flagler Hospital opened January 5, 1921. In the 1930s, the hospital maintained a consistent patient load of sixty to seventy admissions per month. The year 1943 saw the number of patients cared for skyrocket to almost two hundred per month. The hospital expanded over the years, and, in 1989, it moved from Marine Street to a new 75-acre Health Park located on U.S. Highway 1. The old Flagler Hospital structure was demolished and replaced by a condominium. ($5-7)

Condominium, Marine Street, 2008. Flagler Hospital on Marine Street was razed and replaced with "The Views At Baypointe Condominium." The city of St. Augustine is now served by a modern hospital at a different location. Along with the new Flagler Hospital came the Cancer Center, the Heart Center, the Imaging Center, the Spine Center, the Women's Health Center, and the Bariatric Surgery Center.

OLD HOUSE OF DON TOLEDO, AVILES STREET, ST. AUGUSTINE, FLA.

Gaspar Papy House, 36 Aviles Street, 2008.
For years a fanciful tale was woven around this house, but records show Gaspar Papy, one of the colonists who came to St. Augustine from New Smyrna, built it. Since 1928 the house has been owned and used by the Sisters of St. Joseph. The Sisters of St. Joseph own both the Gaspar Papy House and the O'Reilly House, at 32 Aviles Street. The Gaspar Papy House is used for offices. The O'Reilly House is a church related museum, the Father Miguel O'Reilly House. As visitors enter the grounds of the museum, they pass through an authentic historic garden. The garden is located between the Gaspar Papy and O'Reilly houses. The O'Reilly House Museum reflects its Spanish, English, and American heritage spanning over 300 years. In 1725 the house was in the name of Don Lorenzo de Leon. During the Second Spanish Period Father Miguel O'Reilly came to St. Augustine as the parish priest and in 1785 he purchased the house. The O'Reilly House Museum is free and open to the public.

Gaspar Papy House, 36 Aviles Street, 1907.
This house was once advertised as Whitney's Oldest House in the United States. This postcard indicates that Don Toledo built the house in 1516, but records show that Gaspar Papy built the house between 1801 and 1817. John Whitney, a relative of Eli Whitney and friend of Mrs. Abraham Lincoln, operated the "oldest house" and the tourist attractions in the ancient city. His son ran an alligator farm exhibit on Anastasia Island. Free African Americans owned the house during much of the nineteenth century, prior to its incarnation as the oldest house. ($8-10)

Gaspar Papy House, 36 Aviles Street, 1915.
During the early twentieth century, the two-story coquina stone house built in the 1800s by Gaspar Papy was referred to as the Don Toledo House. The house with a low-pitched gable roof, a small overhanging balcony and broad windows with faded red batten shutters, is typical of the houses erected during the Second Spanish Period (1783-1821). It is entered through a side door of the kitchen that opens upon a large room with packed dirt and coquina floor. From the kitchen a jointed wooden stairway, to be drawn up at night, leads to an upstairs bedroom. The house contains relics, antiques, pictures, and furniture used by former residences of the city. ($3-5)

King Street Looking East from Riberia Street, 1907.
Henry M. Flagler wanted King Street, which passed in front of his three grand hotels, to become a broad handsome thoroughfare, uncluttered street. In the early twentieth century Live Oak trees were placed in the street's median. The tower of the Cordova Hotel can be seen in the distance. ($3-5)

King Street Looking East from Riberia Street, 2008.
King Street is now paved, the median is gone, and the tower is now part of the Casa Monica Hotel.

Llambias House, 31 St. Francis Street, 1940s.
Pedro Fernandez built a one-story, two-room house on this site before 1763. The loggia was added during the British Period (1763-1783), and the second floor and balcony during the Second Spanish Period (1783-1821). The Llambias family purchased the house in 1854, occupying it until 1919. Several Llambias children were born in the house. The Llambias House typifies the St. Augustine style, a combination of colonial Spanish, English, and Caribbean building practices that responded to the climate and available local materials. It's sometimes called the Fernandez-Llambias House. Circa 1940s, $3-5.

Llambias House, 31 St. Francis Street, 2008.
The Carnegie Institute, aided by the St. Augustine Historical Society, acquired the property in 1938 and completed restoration of the house in 1954. Architect Stuart Barnette restored the house. The society serves as trustee for the property while the Altrusa Club, an international civic organization, manages the building and spacious grounds. The house is open to the public on the third Sunday of every month. Many legends of the Minorcan Llambias family cling to this ancient Spanish structure.

Marion Hotel, 120 Bay Street, 1930s.
The following advertisement appeared in the 1928 *Foster's Florida Standard Guide*: "Delightfully situated on the Bay, overlooking the Ocean. All modern improvements, private baths, Otis electric elevator, hot and cold running water, steam heat, electric bells and light in every room." ($3-5)

Marion Motor Lodge, 120 Avenida Menendez, 2008.
The Marion Hotel on Avenida Menendez (formerly Bay Street) was razed and replaced with the Marion Motor Lodge.

National Cemetery, 104 Marine Street, 1910.

The National Cemetery, located immediately south of the St. Francis Barracks in St. Augustine, is Florida's oldest national military burial ground. The site has been used for burials since 1818. Most of the burials are soldiers killed in the Second Seminole War, including the victims of the Dade Massacre of December 1835. It is one of ten national cemeteries that display an illuminated flag twenty-four hours a day. The cemetery has been filled since the 1960s. On August 15, 1842, a memorial ceremony was held at the National Cemetery in honor of all the soldiers who died in Florida during the Second Seminole War (1835-1842). Soldiers of all the regiments in the regular Army were represented and wagonloads of bones were buried under a three-pyramid monument. ($3-5)

National Cemetery, 104 Marine Street, 2008.

On December 28, 1835 on the "Military Road" between Fort Brooke (Tampa) and Fort King (Ocala) the detachment of Major Francis L. Dade was ambushed and wiped out by Seminole Indians, which helped set off the Second Seminole War. Six years later on August 14, 1842, Dade's silent command was laid to rest in the National Cemetery in St. Augustine. Visitors to the cemetery will find three stone pyramids that mark the last resting place of those who died in the terrible ambush among the palmetto and pine trees. Later, the tall white obelisk monument was erected in memory of those who died during the Second Seminole War (1835-1842). Sidewalks surround the cemetery, affording visitors a view at any time. The cemetery is located within the grounds of the Florida National Guard preserve.

OLDEST HOUSE IN THE U. S., ST. FRANCIS ST., ST. AUGUSTINE, FLA.

Oldest House, 14 St. Francis Street, 1920s.

The Gonzalez-Alvarez House, known at the "Oldest House" is the area's oldest surviving Spanish colonial house. For more than three centuries the site at 16 St. Francis Street has been occupied by St. Augustinians. Beginning about 1650, successions of thatched wooden structures were their homes. A coquina stone house was built soon after the English burned St. Augustine in 1702, and originally was a one-story rectangle with two rooms. As times changed during the Spanish, British, and American occupations, a wooden second story, an off-street porch, and other features were added. Tomas Gonzalez y Hernandez, an artilleryman at the Castillo de San Marcos, and his family were the next occupants of the house. A Spaniard, Geronimo Alvarez, bought the house in 1790; he and his descendants lived there for about one hundred years. Notable features of the interior include low ceilings, huge fireplaces, crushed coquina floors in the older section, and hand-hewn cedar beams. ($3-5)

Oldest House, 14 St. Francis Street, 2008.

The Oldest House is part of a museum complex owned and operated by the St. Augustine Historical Society since 1918. The society restored the structure to its late eighteenth century glory days. Only the roof was completely replaced. The rooms were furnished with Spanish treasures from the 1600s and 1700s many of which pay tribute to the owners. In 1970, the home was declared a National Historic Landmark. It is open to the public seven days a week. The complex of historical buildings and exhibits include the house museum, the Webb Museum, which offers a panorama of St. Augustine history, the Page Edwards, Jr. Gallery, and the military museum in the Tovar House.

Oldest House Entrance, 1920s. ($1-3)

Oldest House Entrance, 2008.
Today the St. Augustine Historical Society operates its Museum of St. Augustine History in the house.

OLDEST HOUSE GARDEN, ST. AUGUSTINE, FLORIDA—89K

SCOTCH POST OFFICE

Oldest House Garden, 1930s.

The ornamental gardens surrounding the Oldest House featured plants typical of those grown by previous occupants. The displays and plantings fit the surroundings and were very pleasing. The gardens consisted of many plants, flowers, trees, and shrubs. Every turn in the walkway revealed something new to admire. Native plants were used in the landscaping, but there were also many exotic species or varieties adding diversity in shape, texture, and color. Camellias and azaleas were the predominant shrubs throughout the gardens. The walk from the entry gate to the house, especially in the spring, was an unbelievable color experience that dazzled onlookers. Blossoms, blossoms everywhere! ($1-3)

Oldest House Garden, 2008.

A rustic outbuilding, which sits among greenery in the courtyard of the Oldest House, was utilized as an outside kitchen, since cooking was considered to be too dangerous and hot to be done indoors in the early days of the settlement. Some of the trees in the garden include fig trees, mulberry trees, live oaks, cabbage palms, sago palms, and banana trees.

Oldest Store Museum, 4 Artillery Lane, 1940s.
Since the 1880s, this building housed the store of C. F. Hamblen, which by 1908 was Florida's third-largest hardware store. Hamlen later moved and during the 1910s the building was used as a warehouse and garage. The building was eventually transformed into the Oldest Store Museum. There were more than 100,000 items of old general store merchandise on display, including guns, toys, old farm equipment, tools, notions, clothing, early automobile relics, high-wheeled bicycles, butter churns, corsets, sunbonnets, and cracker barrel. The old time general store's shelves were stocked high with calico, derby and straw hats, high-topped shoes, food items, and patent medicines from the 1890s. Out front was a cigar store Indian, a high-wheeled bicycle, an old roasted-peanut wagon, a steam tractor, and a 1927 Model-T Ford. This was the kind of store our ancestors and other residents of that time visited to have their teeth pulled, get a haircut, or spectacles fitted. The museum made visitors realize how far we have come since the days of grandpa's red underwear and the Gibson Girl corset. Most of the items in the store were actually found in the attic of the old store's warehouse. It was here that the first pharmaceutical license in the nation was issued. ($3-5)

Artillery Lofts, 4 Artillery Lane, 2008.
In the 1990s the Oldest Store Museum, with its century old surroundings, was transformed into residential condominium units.

Plaza Hotel and Potter's Wax Museum, 1 King Street, 1950s.
This masonry vernacular building, constructed in 1888, has been used for a variety of commercial businesses. In the 1920s it was a department store. In the 1940s, the Gilbert Hotel and the C. F. Hamblen Hardware Store were located here. From the 1950s to the 1980s it was the Plaza Hotel. In 1949 Potter's Wax Museum, founded by George L. Potter, was located on the first floor of the Plaza Hotel. It is the oldest wax museum in the United States. On display were wax figures of well-known individuals from history, politics, entertainment, science, and other areas. Later the Potter's Wax Museum relocated to 17 King Street, a few doors west of the Plaza Hotel. ($3-5)

Commercial Building, 1 King Street, 2008.
A restaurant and several small commercial businesses are currently occupying this structure that once housed the Plaza Hotel.

Prince Murat House, St. George and Bridge Streets, 1880s.
This quaint and attractive pink, one-and-a-half-story Spanish Colonial period house, built around 1790, is constructed of coquina, a porous, native shell-stone that was quarried on nearby Anastasia Island. The house is plastered to protect the fragile walls from weathering and painted pink, a color that has endured for many years, giving the residence its distinctive character. The house has a pitched roof with two dormer windows on the east façade. Amos Spear added a fancy Victorian balcony with novelty shingle sides, chamfered posts, and jigsaw balustrade around 1880. This unusual architectural feature is the only one of its kind remaining in the city. The house is named for Prince Achille Murat, nephew of Napoleon Bonaparte. Murat arrived in St. Augustine in 1824 and, according to legend, rented this small cottage house. Within two months, he purchased a nearby 1,200-acre plantation. Murat and his wife left St. Augustine in 1836 and eventually retired to Tallahassee, where both are buried. In 1939, when the house was operated as a restaurant, actress Greta Garbo dined there with her companion, Arthur Gaylord Hauser. Seeking a permanent residence in St. Augustine, the house was purchased by Kenneth W. Dow in 1941. Dow furnished the house with antiques associated with the Murat family. Today, the interior reflects Dow's interpretation of the Murat House and the house is now part of the Dow Museum of Historic Houses (formerly Old St. Augustine Village). ($5-7)

Prince Murat House, Dow Museum of Historic Houses, 2008.
The Prince Murat House is now one of nine historic homes that comprise the Dow Museum of Historic Houses located at 149 Cordova Street. These historic homes span the period 1790 to 1910. The first houses on the grounds of the village were built in the early 1600s, but were destroyed in the 1702 attack by British Governor James Moore and his force of eight hundred. The foundations of these early structures lie beneath the village's existing properties. The museum's nine houses, courtyards, and gardens form an entire city block in St. Augustine's oldest historic district. Among the structures are rare Spanish Colonial and Territorial Period houses as well as stately Victorian era homes. Over the centuries, a colorful cast of personalities made its mark on the historic fabric of the museum homes. It was here that Napoleon's favorite nephew befriended noted poet Ralph Waldo Emerson and a royal prince honeymooned with George Washington's grandniece. Nearby, naturalist John Audubon and celebrated author Mark Twain strolled, observing life in nineteenth century St. Augustine. Today these historic homes have been restored to their original splendor and form a microcosm of the Ancient City itself. Dow Museum of Historic Houses is operated by the Museum of Arts and Sciences in Daytona Beach. It was formerly called Old St. Augustine Village.

Spanish Military Hospital, 3 Aviles Street, 1960s.

In the late seventeenth century, a residence on Aviles Street, owned by William Watson, was sold to the Spanish government. This house was then converted to an infirmary and pharmacy. The building became the main hospital (Spanish Military Hospital) in 1818, when fire destroyed the one across the street. This building was demolished in 1880. Over the years several businesses operated at this location until the Historic St. Augustine Preservation board, in 1967, reconstructed the old Spanish Military Hospital. ($5-7)

Spanish Military Hospital, 3 Aviles Street, 2008.

See what a hospital looked like 250-years ago. The Spanish Military Hospital represents an early Spanish hospital and offers glimpses into early medicine in the ancient city. See the doctor's office where operations were performed. All furnishings except the bed are eighteenth century antique. Today the hospital building also serves as an office for "ghost tours" of St. Augustine.

Spear Mansion, St. George Street, 1920s.

The Spear Mansion was the winter home of Amos C. Spear. The mansion and carriage house (now part of the Dow Museum of Historic Homes) were built by John Howard, Spear's father-in-law, after the Civil War (1861-1865). In the late 1800s, Spear owned not only the mansion, but also all of the houses and properties that today comprise the Dow Museum of Historic Houses (formerly the Old St. Augustine Village). By 1910, a second story was added to the Spear Mansion. By 1920, the house was operated as the Spear Mansion Hotel, which had accommodations for one hundred guests. It was open all year and the proprietress was Mrs. A. R. Spencer. ($18-20)

Sisters of St. Joseph Motherhouse, 241 St. George Street, 2008.

The Spear Mansion Hotel was torn down and replaced by the parking lot north of the Dow Museum of Historic Homes and other property owned by the sisters of St. Joseph. The St. George Street Motherhouse is an enduring landmark. Exterior lines tell the French origin of Sister-builders while the modern interior leans to future needs. The Motherhouse remains today a fostering and coordinating center for their statewide apostolic ministries.

St. Augustine, Fla. St. Francis Barracks & Monastery.

St. Francis Barracks, 82 Marine Street, 1907.
The coquina walls of the St. Francis Barracks were once part of the Franciscan chapel and friary of Our Lady of the Immaculate Conception established by missionaries from Spain. Before these walls were built, thatched-roofed wooden buildings on the site were burned in 1599, rebuilt, and again destroyed by fire in 1702 when Governor James Moore of Carolina led a two-month siege on St. Augustine. The barracks were used by the British during their occupation (1763-1783) and by the Spanish until Florida became U.S. Territory in 1821. In 1821 the U.S. Army took over the complex and used the old cells as a jail. ($15-17)

Florida National Guard, 82 Marine Street, 2008.
The complex was leased to the Florida National Guard in 1907 and formally given to them in 1921 by an Act of Congress. The St. Francis Barracks is a two-story, yellow, stucco building with a shallow balconied court, topped with a flat balustrade. Officially designated as a military barracks in 1881, it houses the State arsenal and executive offices of the Florida National Guard. The main building, gutted by fire in 1915, was restored in 1921. The building forms the centerpiece of a complex of military buildings whose historical origins span three centuries of St. Augustine's history and includes one other Colonial-era building, the King's Bakery, built by the British, and several residences that date from the late nineteenth century Victorian era.

St. Francis Inn, 279 St. George Street, 1880s.

This Second Spanish Period (1783-1821) house was first owned by Gaspar Garcia, a sergeant in the Third Battalion of the Infantry Regiment of Cuba. In 1802, sea captain Juan Ruggiers purchased it. Colonel Thomas Henry Dummett, a planter and officer in the British marines, established the Dummett Plantation in 1825. This plantation, located on the Tomoka River, near present-day Ormond Beach, became a productive plantation with a Sugar Mill and Rum Distillery. The ruins of this plantation are still standing in the forest north of Ormond Beach. In 1835, when Seminole Indians took to war, Dummett moved his family to St. Augustine for safety and the Dummett Plantation was destroyed by the Seminoles. Two years later, the Colonel purchased the St. Augustine house built in 1791. This structure has been a public guesthouse since 1845. That was the year Mary, widow of Colonel Thomas Henry Dummett, conveyed the house and lot to their daughters Anna and Sarah. The Dummett House prospered through a succession of owners, name changes, and improvements. Philanthropist John L. Wilson purchased the inn in 1888 and made extensive renovations, adding a third floor and the mansard roof. In the 1920s central heating and bathrooms were installed. Through the years the inn was known as the Dummett House, Dummett-Hardee House, Teahan House, Hudson House, Valencia Annex, Amity Apartments, Salt Air Apartments, Palms, and Graham House. It became the St. Francis Inn in 1948. ($5-7)

St. Francis Street and Oldest House
St. Augustine, Florida

St. Francis Street Looking West from Marine Street, 1824.

St. Francis Street takes its name from the Franciscan monastery that once occupied the southeast side of the street. This engraving depicts the street in 1874. The Gonzalez-Alvarez House (Oldest House) and Tovar House are on the right. The Llambias House is on the left. Cancelled 1954, $2-4.

St. Francis Inn, 279 St. George Street, 2008.

A narrow, uneven brick road leads guests to one of the oldest inns in St. Augustine. The St. Francis Inn surrounds its guests with history dating back to the Second Spanish Period (1783-1821) when the structure was first built. The inn faces a courtyard and sub-tropical gardens and has a variety of single and double rooms, two- and three-room suites, and a five-room cottage that was once the slave quarters. The fireplace, wainscoting, and stairs are all original. The downstairs features a full kitchen, sitting room that opens onto the courtyard, and a small pool. Banana trees, bougainvillea, fragrant jasmine, and other exotic flora shade the garden. Stepping through the wrought-iron fence and under the archway into the St. Francis Inn is like taking a delightful trip back in time. Some believe this Inn is haunted by the ghost of Lily, a black maid who fell in love with the white son of General William J. Hardee, who owned the structure. According to legend, the son hung himself when their relationship was forbidden and Lily continues to inhabit the site.

St. Francis Street Looking West from Marine Street, 2008.

St. George Hotel, St. Augustine, Fla.—6

St. George Hotel, St. George Street, circa 1915.
During the 1880s the home of General Peter Skenandoah Smith was remodeled and converted to the St. George Hotel. It was located next to Trinity Episcopal Church in downtown St. Augustine and razed during World War II. ($3-5)

St. George Hotel Site, St. George Street, 2008.
The St. George Hotel was torn down and the site is now a parking lot for the Trinity Episcopal Church.

Tovar House, 22 St. Francis Street, 1910s.
The infantryman Jose Tovar lived on this corner in 1763. The original site and size of his house remained unchanged during the British Period (1763-1783) when John Johnson, a Scottish merchant, lived here. After the Spanish returned to Florida in 1783, Jose Coruna, a Canary Islander, his family, and Tomas Caraballo, an assistant surgeon, occupied the house. Geronimo Alvarez lived next door in the Gonzalez-Alvarez House and purchased the property in 1791. It remained in his family until 1871. A later occupant was Civil War General Martin D. Hardin. The St. Augustine Historical Society has owned the Tovar House since 1918. ($5-7)

Tovar House, 22 St. Francis Street, 2008.
The Tovar House is used by the St. Augustine Historical Society to display photographs and artifacts relating to Florida's military, including soldiers of various periods, their belongings, and weapons. A ticket to the Gonzalez-Alvarez House, or Oldest House, includes entry to the Tovar House.

Trinity Episcopal Church, St. Augustine, Fla.

The Oldest City in the United States

VILLA FLORA, ST. AUGUSTINE, FLA.

Trinity Episcopal Church, St. George and King Streets, 1930s.
Florida's oldest Protestant church, Trinity Episcopal Church, dates back to 1821. The cornerstone was laid June 23, 1825. The church is an unostentatious example of Gothic Revival architecture. During its lifetime, the church has had many rectors, including Rev. Frances Huger Rutledge, who became the first Episcopal Bishop of Florida. Prior to the Civil War, Rev. Benjamin Whipple was the rector for a short while. He was known as the "Apostle of the Indians" as he frequently visited nearby plantations. Once Whipple became so upset at the treatment of the Seminole Indians that he went to the Federal Government and asked them to stop the hanging of Seminole Indian leaders. The church was renovated in 1904, with additions being added on since then. ($3-5)

Villa Flora, 234 St. George Street, circa 1915.
Built by Reverend O. A. Weenolson as a "winter cottage" in 1898, this coquina and yellow brick structure is one of a few in St. Augustine with a raised basement. The structure contains extensive stained glasswork. Its name stems from the beautiful flower garden originally maintained next to the structure. In 1906 Alanson Wood, one of the inventors of the roller coaster, purchased it. After his death, his widow ran it as a small hotel. In the 1920s and 1930s it became a restaurant. ($3-5)

Villa Flora, 234 St. George Street, 2008.
The design of this Moorish-Romanesque Revival house is a splendid example of a Flagler era "winter cottage." It was probably inspired by the design of Franklin Smith's Villa Zorayda. The cottage later served as a hotel, restaurant, and gift shop. In 1940, the Sisters of St. Joseph, whose convent is across St. George Street, bought Villa Flora and used it as a schoolroom and residence for the nuns.

Trinity Episcopal Church, St. George and King Streets, 2008.
The present structure is a combination of the old and the new, containing only a small part of the original building. The King Street façade and a portion of the east wall behind the baptistery are the original walls fashioned of "hewn stones," or coquina. The Italian marble front dates back to 1890. The cypress single spire remains unchanged. Archaeologists in recent years have discovered the oldest well site in North America and the site of a small house, which was occupied by a Spanish soldier and his wife. The church hopes to rebuild these structures as they once stood and open them to the public. Louis C. Tiffany did the stained glass window in the chapel.

King Street showing Ponce de Leon,
St. Augustine, Fla.

Transportation: Streetcars, King Street, 1907.

A streetcar railway that headed for the south beach area on Anastasia Island ran from King Street over a wooden trestle bridge (South Beach Bridge) to the vicinity of the Alligator Farm. The line, operated by George Reddington, was known as the "Old Dummy line." Henry M. Flagler fought to keep a trolley from being run down this main road. Many people in town saw the trolley as a needed transportation link between the older part of town and the new western sections, but Flagler disagreed. He wanted King Street, which passed in front of his three hotels, to become a broad, handsome thoroughfare, uncluttered by unsightly tracks and trolley cars. He argued that carriages could easily handle east-west traffic. ($13-20)

Transportation: Tourist Trolleys, King Street, 2008.
Today the electric streetcars have been replaced with trolley vehicles that travel a seven-mile historical route through the ancient city.

Old Aviles Street (Spanish Quarter) 22
St. Augustine, Florida

Fatio House

Ximenez-Fatio House, 20 Aviles Street, 1930s.

The oldest inn in Florida still in existence in its original form is the Ximenez-Fatio House, located at 20 Aviles Street. It was built by Andres Ximenez, a Spanish merchant, in 1798 as a private residence and grocery store. After Ximenez's death in 1806, the structure passed through several hands. In 1830 a widow named Margaret Cook bought the property and turned it into a boarding house—one of the few acceptable business ventures for nineteenth century women. Eight guestrooms held up to twenty-three visitors, including the speculators, sea captains, and invalids who flowed into Florida at the time. In 1836, Sarah Anderson, a plantation owner in the Daytona Beach area, purchased the house and lived there for almost twenty years. In 1855 Louisa Fatio purchased the house. By that time an ell and balcony had been added and the house was operating as an inn. It continued as an inn for twenty years. When Miss Fatio died in 1875, the property passed to her nephew, David L. Dunham, and the house was rented out until the National Society of the Colonial Dames of America purchased it in 1939. Since then it has been open to the public as a historic exhibit. ($3-5)

Ximenez-Fatio House, 20 Aviles Street, 2008.

The house is now a public museum maintained by the Florida branch of the Colonial Dames of America, with the building preserved as it was during Florida's Territorial Period (1821-1845) when the area's tourism industry began. In the 1980s the building and grounds were restored. Its old slave quarters, Spanish kitchen, patio, and balconies are of interest to visitors. Today's tourists will delight to see how their traveling predecessors "roughed it" without the luxuries associated with modern vacation accommodations. They can readily see the advantages of being in a world where time passed slowly and one could enjoy a week or a month of strolling among the orange trees, relaxing in such a civilized place as this old St. Augustine inn.

Worth House, 16 Marine Street, 1910s.

Miguel Ysnardy built this house in 1791 during the Second Spanish Period (1783-1821). It operated as a hotel before the Civil War. The house was later purchased by Margaret S. Worth, widow of General William J. Worth, veteran of the Seminole Indian and Mexican Wars. Thereafter it became known simply as the Worth House. The Worth family owned the house from 1817 to 1869, operating it as the Union Hotel from 1819 to 1830. In 1915 the structure was owned by H. J. Usina and advertised (as indicated in this view) as the "oldest house in America." Usina claimed that the house dated back to 1588. In 1960 the old structure was razed. ($3-5)

The Oldest House in America, St. Augustine, Fla.—8
(On The Bay Front.)

O. C. White's Seafood & Spirits, 118 Avenida Menendez, 2008.

The historic Worth House was demolished in 1960 and a reconstruction using the original coquina walls was built on a lot bounded by Marine Street and Avenida Menendez. The occupant of this new structure is O. C. White's Seafood & Spirits restaurant and tavern.

Ancient City Baptist Church, 30 Carrera Street, Circa 1895.
Henry Flagler donated land for the Ancient City Baptist Church, which was established in 1887, and the first services were held in the new building February 10, 1895. The style of architecture is Romanesque Revival, with a cone shaped turret on top of a three-story tower. President and Mrs. Warren G. Harding attended the morning worship service on February 19, 1921. Since 1955 the church's members have served students at the Florida State School for the Deaf and Blind in St. Augustine. ($5-7)

Ancient City Baptist Church, 30 Carrera Street, 2008.
The Ancient City Baptist Church has grown and seen many pastors who have made a name for themselves. There was Rev. K. W. Cawthon, who went to Argentina as a missionary; Rev. James E. Cates served as pastor for two five-year periods; Rev. Alber E. Calkins was the pastor for nineteen years; and Dr. J. L. Rosser spent nine years as pastor. He was a distinguished scholar who wrote for a number of Southern Baptist publications. Dr. Rosser wrote a "History of Florida Baptist," the first publication of this kind.

THE BARCELONA HOTEL, ST. AUGUSTINE, FLORIDA

1389

Barcelona Hotel, Carrera and Seville Streets, 1920s.
Henry Ball, a New York businessman, built a large home in 1874 on the corner of Sevilla and Valencia streets. In the late 1880s, Henry Flagler had the house moved one block, to the corner of Sevilla and Carerra Streets, and converted into the Barcelona Hotel. A 1928 *Foster's Florida Standard Guide* advertisement reads, "The Barcelona Hotel opens wide its hospitable doors to its old and new friends—to those who love comfort—best of foods—and an atmosphere only found in a very large private home—filled with art treasures—beautiful rugs—soft lights and sunny, well-furnished bedrooms—and a quiet air of refinement. With all the atmosphere of an old Southern Mansion." ($2-4)

Flagler College, 74 King Street, 1968.
Formerly the Ponce de Leon Hotel built by Henry M. Flagler in 1888, it is acclaimed as one of the finest examples of Spanish Renaissance architecture in America. In 1968 the hotel was turned into Flagler College, a four-year co-educational liberal arts college. ($2-4)

Flagler College, 74 King Street, 2008.
The centerpiece of the Flagler College campus is the former Ponce de Leon Hotel. The college's impressive dining hall and rotunda feature murals by George Maynard and stained glass windows by Louis Comfort Tiffany.

Barcelona Hotel Site, Carrera and Seville Streets, 2008.
Over the years Barcelona Hotel was modified and enlarged. Razed in 1962, the site is now a parking lot for the Ancient City Baptist Church.

Florida East Coast Railway Buildings, Riberia Street, Circa 1983.
Henry Flagler bought several northeast Florida railroads at the same time he started building the Ponce de Leon and Alcazar hotels in St. Augustine, marking the beginning of the Florida East Coast (FEC) Railway. Eventually, he extended the FEC down the east coast of Florida, first reaching Palm Beach and then Miami in 1896. The building was the office for the president and other officers of the FEC system. Construction started in 1923 and was completed in December 1925. ($1-3)

Flagler College Buildings, Riberia Street, 2008.
The Florida East Coast Railway Buildings were purchased by Flagler College and were remodeled for use as offices and student dormitories.

Grace United Methodist Church, 8 Carrera Street, 1960s.
Grace United Methodist Church was founded by George L. Atkins and Sons, who owned the Florida House Hotel on St. George Street. Built in 1887, it features salmon colored surfaces, cast terra-cotta decorations, with exposed concrete and shell aggregate. This Spanish Renaissance church was built by John M. Carrere and Thomas Hastings, the architects and builders of Flagler Memorial Presbyterian Church and Ponce de Leon Hotel. ($1-3)

Grace United Methodist Church, 8 Carrera Street, 2008.
Grace United Methodist was formerly known as Olivet Methodist Episcopal Church, a wooden building that stood on the site and was later used to build Henry Flagler's Alcazar Hotel. Grace United Methodist Church is an active house of worship. A room in the church contains photographs and documents relating to the history of the building. In the same area of St. Augustine are the Flagler Memorial Presbyterian Church and the Ancient City Baptist Church, all three the result of Henry Flagler's generosity.

Old Drug Store, 31 Orange Street, 1940s.
T. W. Speissigger and Sons entered the pharmacy business in 1875. Their drug store opened in 1887 and carried medicine, miletries, and tobacco. The business was continued by the sons into the 1960s. The old wooden store was then converted into the Old Drug Store Museum. ($1-3)

Old Drug Store, 31 Orange Street, 2008.
Today the Old Drug Store is a free attraction supported by gift shop sales.

Memorial (Presbyterian) Church, St. Augustine, Fla.

Flagler Memorial Presbyterian Church, 36 Valencia Street, 1930s.

This Venetian Renaissance church was completed in 1890. Its architecture and elegant interior décor reflect the period of the "golden age" of the late 1800s and turn of the twentieth century. This structure in yellow and white terra cotta and yellow brick, topped with a copper dome that is more than one hundred feet in height, is built in the shape of a Latin cross. Mosaic floors are of Siena marble, relieved by plaques of breccia violet marble. Architects Carrere and Hastings of New York and European craftsmen imported in great numbers for the work combined to erect, in record time, a church of such beauty that it's frequently called the Cathedral of North Florida. Henry Flagler built it in memory of his daughter Jennie Louise Benedict, who died of childbirth complications. Flagler, his wife, daughter, and granddaughter are buried in an attached mausoleum. ($3-5)

Flagler Memorial Presbyterian Church, 36 Valencia Street, 2008.

The Flagler Memorial Presbyterian Church, located on the northeast corner of Valencia and Sevilla Streets, is open to the public. A guide is available seven days a week to explain the history and architecture of the building. Church services are held on Sunday mornings.

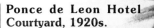

70210   THE COURT OF THE PONCE DE LEON, ST. AUGUSTINE, FLA.   COPR. DETROIT PUBLISHING CO.

Ponce de Leon Hotel Courtyard, 1920s.
Tourists relax in the courtyard of the opulent Ponce de Leon Hotel. The vine-clad verandas were surrounded by handsomely landscaped grounds. By the early twentieth century, ladies in the Ponce de Leon courtyard were wearing more casual dresses and hemlines were rising just a little. ($4-6)

Flagler College Courtyard, 2008.
Visitors entering Flagler College walk through the courtyard, past the fountain, and under a terra cotta archway.

Front Entrance to Ponce de Leon Hotel, St. Augustine, Fla.

Ponce de Leon Hotel, 75 King Street, Circa 1910.

As part of the development of St. Augustine into a stylish winter resort, entrepreneur Henry Flagler commissioned young New York architect Thomas Hastings (later a partner in the firm of Carrere and Hastings) to design Ponce de Leon Hotel in 1887. Modeled after a Moorish castle, the hotel was adorned with domes, spires, turrets, and fountains. Its interior was decorated with Louis C. Tiffany stained glass mosaics and terra-cotta relief. It had two miles of corridors and covered most of a five-acre lot. The exterior walls, four feet thick, were made of poured concrete. The furnishings in each of the 450 rooms and suites were worth about $1,000, which was a lot of money in the 1880s. For the convenience of wealthy winter visitors, he extended train service from northern cities on the Florida East Coast Railway to what was being heralded as the "Newport of the South." Ponce de Leon Hotel opened in 1888, the first of Flagler's chain of Florida East Coast hotels, and established St. Augustine as a fashionable winter resort. In the 1960s, the Ponce de Leon Hotel became Flagler College. ($2-6)

Flagler College, 75 King Street, 2008.
Flagler College opened its doors September 24, 1968. Visitors marvel at the beautiful terra cotta and coquina structure. Named in honor of oil magnate, developer, and philanthropist Henry Morrison Flagler, the college is a living museum and unique representation of Spanish Renaissance Revival architecture, lovingly preserved and listed on the National Register of Historic Places. Featuring a small student-to-teacher ratio, a campus that is one of the most beautiful in the country, and a wide range of academic majors, its nineteen-acre campus lies in the heart of historic St. Augustine.

LOGIA OF HOTEL PONCE DE LEON, ST. AUGUSTINE, FLA.

Front and Main Entrance, Hotel Ponce De Leon, St. Augustine, Fla.

Ponce de Leon Hotel Logia, circa 1915.
The roofed-open gallery of the Ponce de Leon was a favorite lounging place for guests during concert performances in the court. The wide-arched verandas flanked the courtyard. ($1-3)

Flagler College Logia, 2008.

Ponce de Leon Hotel Main Entrance, Circa 1910.
Facing south from this doorway offered a full view of the magnificence of the courtyard. The doorway opened into the rotunda from the court. ($4-6)

Flagler College Main Entrance, 2008.

Tolomato Cemetery, 10 Cordova Street, 1930s.

During the First Spanish Period, prior to 1763 the Christian Indian Village of Tolomato occupied this site, with Franciscan missionaries serving its chapel and burying ground. The village was abandoned when England acquired Florida. In 1777 Father Pedro Camps, pastor of the Minorcan colonies who had come to St. Augustine after the failure of Andrew Turnbull's settlement at New Smyrna, obtained permission from Governor Patrick Tonym to establish this cemetery for his parishioners. Father Camps was buried here in 1790; ten years later his remains were re-interred in the new church, the present cathedral. The last burial took place in 1892. ($1-3)

Tolomato Cemetery, 10 Cordova Street, 2008.

A secure fence surrounds Tolomato Cemetery, which is visible from the sidewalk along Cordova Street. The cemetery is closed to the public. The mortuary chapel on the grounds contains the remains of the Most Reverend Jean Pierre Augustin Marcellin Verot, the first bishop of St. Augustine, who died in 1876. In 1859, Bishop Verot established the city's Convent School, predecessor of the present St. Joseph's Academy.

Y.M.C.A., 59 Valencia Street, Circa 1910.

In 1908 a redbrick Y.M.C.A. building was constructed with a clay tile roof and thick carved rafters. The structure included a swimming pool, gymnasium, and a bowling alley. Henry Flagler and the Florida East Coast Railway Athletic Association financially supported the construction, however, members were expected to pay dues. The building of the Y.M.C.A. was especially important because it was open year-round as opposed to the Alcazar's Casino that was only open during the winter season. ($3-5)

Flagler College Tennis Courts, 59 Valencia Street, 2008.

Flagler College purchased the Y.M.C.A. site and converted it into tennis courts. This building contains the school's tennis association offices.

Chapter Eight

Southwest of the Plaza

The Front Towers, Hotel Alcazar, St. Augustine, Fla.

Alcazar Hotel Court, Circa 1908.
This view shows the Alcazar Court looking through to King Street. Adaptations from famous Moorish buildings in Spain were incorporated into the Alcazar, which blended beautifully with its garden settings. The great central court, which was one mass of foliage, could be viewed as hotel visitors dined. This view was taken before the addition of the fourth floor. ($4-6)

Lightner Museum Court, 2008.
This view of the Lightner Museum courtyard shows the fourth floor windows and rooftop balustrade.

Alcazar Hotel Front Towers, Circa 1910.
With its two large towers ornate spires and red tile roofs, the Alcazar Hotel reflected its Arabic name. ($4-6)

Alcazar Hotel Courtyard Bridge, 1910s. ($1-3)

Lightner Museum Courtyard Bridge, 2008.
In the courtyard of the Lightner Museum, a stone footbridge offers a path over a pond and into a lush garden.

Lightner Museum Front Towers, 2008.
Today visitors walk through these two massive towers to visit the old hotel courtyard and the Lightner Museum.

6225 THE ALCAZAR, ST. AUGUSTINE, FLA.

Alcazar Hotel, 79 King Street, 1910.
The Spanish Renaissance Revival style Alcazar Hotel was Henry Flagler's second luxury hotel. The royal palace in Seville, Spain inspired the design by architects Carrere and Hastings. The Alcazar featured a courtyard, steam baths, gardens, a gymnasium, massage parlors, fountains, a casino, ballrooms, and the world's largest indoor swimming pool. Early in the twentieth century a bridge connected the Alcazar and Cordova hotels over Cordova Street. Alcazar Hotel was sold when the area's tourism began declining. ($3-5)

Lightner Museum, 79 King Street, 2008.

In 1947, wealthy Chicago publisher Otto C. Lightner purchased the former Alcazar Hotel for $150,000 ending his search for a location to house his extensive collection of Victorian memorabilia, including pottery, stained glass, musical instruments, paintings, crystal bowls, and just about everything else he collected on his world travels. In 1950 Lightner bequeathed the building and his extravagant collection to the City of St. Augustine. A million dollar restoration project returned the structure to a grand illustrious architectural treasure. Today, Lightner Museum boasts hundreds of collections numbering more than 20,000 individual items and three floors of exhibits catering to all kinds of interests. It's one of the most preeminent museums on Florida's East Coast.

The Lightner Museum stands in the center of St. Augustine as a reminder of the Gilded Era. The architectural vision of Henry Flagler and the many collections of Otto Lightner bring to life a simpler time when there were fewer distractions to prevent people from enjoying the finer things in life. The former hotel was added to the National Register of Historic Places in 1971. In the north courtyard is a statue of Pedro Menendez, erected in 1972. It was a gift from Aviles, Spain, and the garden was dedicated as the Parque de Menendez in 1979. Today a portion of the old Alcazar Hotel houses the St. Augustine City Hall.

Swimming Pool, Alcazar Casino, St. Augustine, Fla.—38

Alcazar Casino Swimming Pool, 1924.
The Alcazar Hotel swimming pool was, at the time, the largest indoor pool in the world. The Alcazar Casino was located south of the main hotel structure. Artesian well water entered the Casino pool from below while sunshine entered from a skylight above. The pool was so extravagant that the water extended into the dressing areas. Men could access the main pool by diving underwater while the ladies' side was closed off so they could swim in private. The pool was 125-feet long, 50-feet wide, and three to twelve feet deep. The Alcazar Casino overlooking the famous Alcazar pool was a great hideout for a hearty game of poker, a stiff drink, and an aromatic Cuban cigar. Cancelled 1924, $10-12.

Lightner Antique Mall, 2008.
The Lightner Antique Mall is uniquely placed in the renovated swimming pool of the old Alcazar Hotel. The mall-like environment features shops specializing in antiques and collectibles, as well as a café.

Alcazar Hotel Tennis Courts, 1891.
These tennis courts were located south of the Alcazar Casino. At the left of this view are the Buckingham Hotel and Villa Zorayda. *This photograph is from Picturesque St. Augustine by Edward Bierstadt, 1891.*

Buckingham Hotel, 12 Granada Street, Circa 1910.
The Buckingham Hotel was located directly opposite the Ponce de Leon and Alcazar hotels. It had beautiful grounds, large verandas, and sun parlors. Buckingham Hotel was initially created as a haven for destitute African-Americans, supported by a bequest from Buckingham Smith. After Smith's death in 1871, the Buckingham Smith Benevolent Association was formed and provided charitable works for over one hundred years. Hand-colored postcard. ($5-7)

Lightner Museum Mall Parking Lot, 2008.
The old Alcazar Hotel tennis courts now serve as a parking lot for the Lightner Museum and the City of St. Augustine.

Flagler College Gymnasium, 12 Granada Street, 2008.
The Flagler College Gymnasium occupies the Buckingham Hotel site.

Carcaba Cigar Factory, 88 Riberia Street, Circa 1898.

P. F. Carcaba, a native of Oviedo, Spain, founded the P. F. Carcaba & Co. Cigar Factory. Carcaba brought his cigar making business from Cincinnati, Ohio to St. Augustine in 1893 and began producing Havana "Caballeros," whose boxes featured pictures of Henry Flagler's great hotels. The original cigar factory building was later replaced by a new building that operated as a cigar factory until the collapse of the Florida economy in 1926. ($5-7)

Office Building, 88 Riberia Street, 2008.

A succession of businesses occupied the old cigar factory building before its restoration in 1985. This privately owned commercial office building is the last remnant of the cigar industry in St. Augustine.

118

Granada Hotel, King and Granada Streets, 1907.
The Granada Hotel was located on King Street beside Villa Zorayda and across from the Ponce de Leon Hotel. Cancelled 1907, $8-10.

Wachovia Bank, King and Granada Streets, 2008.
Wachovia Bank and other businesses now occupy the site of the former Granada Hotel. To the right of the bank is the Villa Zorayda.

Granada Hotel and Villa Zorayda, King Street, 1911.
This view of King Street shows a horse-drawn carriage in front of the Granada Hotel and Villa Zorayda. Cancelled 1911, $8-10.

Wachovia Bank and Villa Zorayda, King Street, 2008.
Granada Hotel was replaced with buildings occupied by other businesses including Wachovia Bank. The Villa Zorayda is on the right.

S. A. 77—Villa Zorayda, St. Augustine, Florida

Villa Zorayda, 83 King Street, 1920s.
Villa Zorayda, a vine-covered coquina and concrete structure of Moorish design, was trimmed in bright red, blue, and yellow, the Moorish colors. The house was erected in 1883 by Boston architect Franklin W. Smith, who based his design on a portion of the famed Alhambra Castle in Spain. Smith had a large collection of inlaid and elaborately carved Oriental pieces, ancient Egyptian hangings, valuable rugs, and ancient firearms. In 1913 Abraham S. Mussallem purchased the Villa Zorayda, adding his collection of valuable and rare furnishings obtained while serving as Egyptian consulate. ($1-3)

The Zorayda Club, St. Augustine, Fla.

Zorayda Club, 83 King Street, Circa 1923.
From 1922 to 1925 Villa Zorayda was used as the Zorayda Club, a nightclub and gambling casino. The club closed when Florida outlawed gambling. In 1936, it opened as a tourist attraction called Zorayda Castle. ($5-7)

Villa Zorayda, 83 King Street, 2008.
Since 1936 the Mussallem family operated the building as a tourist attraction, Zorayda Castle. Zorayda Castle closed to the public in 1998 and the building was unoccupied for several years. It is open today as Villa Zorayda, a museum of elaborately carved Oriental pieces, ancient Egyptian hangings, valuable rugs, and ancient firearms. The building's flamboyant architecture is easily viewed from King Street.

Chapter Nine

Anastasia Island

St. Augustine, Fla. old Anastasia Island.

Anastasia Island, 1908.
Boasting twenty-four miles of sun-soaked shores, the beaches of Anastasia Island feature twenty-foot sand dunes with sabal palms and sea oats that grow wild along the Atlantic coastline. Shelling for sand dollars, moon snails, and angel wings was as easy as picking them up off the sand. The first conflict for the newly constructed lighthouse was the Spanish-American War (April 22 to December 10, 1898). Well before an official declaration, the U.S. began preparing the Florida Coast, fearing Spain would try to regain its former territory. In April 1898, engineers began constructing fortifications and brought a cannon to the light station. ($5-7)

Anastasia Island, 2008.
There is perhaps no other beach area in Florida that offers such a variety of sights and activities. One minute one can be strolling a deserted shore as a whale surfaces nearby, the next one can be climbing a colonial fort, hanging ten with surfers, or driving a car on a sandy beach.

Fort Matanzas, 1890s.
Once decayed and crumbling, this old landmark bears mute testimony of that historic period when the Spaniards were heroically struggling to defend St. Augustine against the invader. Militant English colonists were a constant menace and the fort was primarily built to repel a possible attack from that "back door" quarter. Fort Matanzas was erected between the years 1740-1742. Just inside Matanzas Inlet, on Rattlesnake Island, it is eighteen miles south of the Castillo de San Marcos and St. Augustine. Today it is a National Monument. ($3-5)

Fort Matanzas, 2008.
Fort Matanzas, completed by the Spanish in 1742 as a fortress against British colonial invasion, can be explored every day of the year except Christmas. In addition to the fort, the surrounding park has a mile of beach and nature trails. Fort Matanzas is now a National Monument, preserved and supervised by the National Park Service of the U.S. Department of Interior.

St. Augustine Watchtower, Anastasia Island, 1898.
The Spanish erected this stone watchtower at the entrance to Matanzas Bay in the mid-1700s. Subsequently, the British and then the Americans made improvements, including the 1823 change to a lighthouse. During the Civil War, Confederates removed the light's lenses to deny its use to Union forces soon to occupy St. Augustine. With coastal erosion threatening the first lighthouse, Congress started work on the current lighthouse in 1871. Construction took three years. ($5-7)

Lighthouse, Anastasia Island, 1920s.
In 1871 Congress appropriated $60,000 for the construction of a new lighthouse. On October 15, 1874, the light atop the new tower was lit and the light on the weakening shoulders of the old Spanish watchtower was permanently extinguished. William W. Russell, the lighthouse keeper, had 219 winding steps of cast iron to ascend to the top within the 165-foot tall tower painted a spiraling black and white with a bright red top. The lighthouse lamp was originally lit by lard oil, illuminating a rotating first-order Frensel lens. ($1-3)

ANASTASIA LIGHTHOUSE, NEAR ST. AUGUSTINE

Lighthouse, Anastasia Island, 2008.
Most roads to old St. Augustine were sea lanes, and lighthouses have always been a part of this town's landscape. A 1586 map of the town shows a lighthouse or watchtower on Anastasia Island across Matanzas Bay from the Castillo de San Marcos. The relentless pounding of the sea caused more than one lighthouse to be replaced during the past four hundred years. The present lighthouse, on the National Register of Historic Places, still guides ships in the area. 219 steps to the top—one breathtaking view! Visitors can climb to the top of this 165-foot-high working lighthouse for spectacular views of the city, beaches, and the nation's oldest port. The Lighthouse Museum contains photographs and artifacts of St. Augustine's maritime past as well as early life at the lighthouse.

Top Deck Crowd at Marine Studios

Marineland, 1940s.
An aerial view of Marineland, the world's first Oceanarium, located on U.S. Highway A1A between the Atlantic Ocean and Florida's Inland Waterway (Matanzas River). Fish live in two huge tanks connected by a flume. The tanks are maintained to approximate conditions of marine life in the open sea. High jumping bottlenose dolphins, or porpoises as they are commonly called, are known and beloved by mariners. These friendly air-breathing, warm-blooded mammals were first introduced into prolonged captivity at Marineland, which opened in 1938 and was added to the National Historic Register in 1986. ($3-5)

D-221 Feeding Time at Marine Studio, Marineland, Fla.

Marineland OF FLORIDA

Marineland, 2008.
Today, there are no scheduled dolphin shows at Marineland; however, visitors can have personal encounters with dolphins in their 1.3-million gallon habitat. People of all ages have the opportunity to swim and play with the animals in a way usually reserved for trainers, or simply enjoy watching other guests play with the dolphins.

Sand Dunes, Circa 2004.
Along much of the coast of North America stretch barrier islands, long, narrow strips of sand built up over time by ocean currents, waves, and wind. Anastasia Island is a barrier island. Facing the ocean are sand dunes covered by hardy plants such as sea oats and beach sunflower. The deep roots of sea oats and other grasses help hold the dunes in place. Just behind the dunes is an area of coastal scrub consisting of other salt-tolerant plants such as sabal palm, saw palmetto and scrub live oak. ($1-3)

Sand Dunes, 2008.
Towering 10,000-year-old sand dunes along with sea winds and white-capped waves offer visitors an exhilarating day at the beach.

REDDINGTON'S "GATOR" FARM, FLORIDA.

South Beach Alligator Farm, Anastasia Island, 1911.

Alligators were first used to attract visitors to a small museum and souvenir shop on St. Augustine Beach at the terminus of a trolley railway that ran across the South Beach Bridge and south on Anastasia Island. The owners soon discovered the public's fascination with the reptiles and in 1909 incorporated the South Beach Alligator Farm and Museum of Marine Curiosities, which they moved to its present location in 1920. The men who first saw the alligators as a tourist attraction in 1893 were Felix Fire and George Reddington. W. I. Drysdale and F. Charles Usina purchased ownership in 1936 and, after a disastrous fire, began at once to rebuild the facilities, expand the collection, and create national publicity for the attraction. The farm was renamed the St. Augustine Alligator Farm. ($3-5)

St. Augustine Alligator Farm, Circa 1945.

The St. Augustine Alligator Farm is one of the oldest continuously operated attractions created specifically for the purpose of entertaining visitors. Thousands of servicemen who visited the Alligator Farm during World War II helped to broadcast its popularity. The collection of alligators and other animals in a controlled environment has provided a unique opportunity for scientists to conduct research in cooperation with the institution. The St. Augustine Alligator Farm's role in the development of tourism in the state was recognized in 1992 with its listing on the National Register of Historic Places. The "Mission" style main building of the Alligator farm, shown here, has been a landmark along U.S. Highway A1A for more than seventy years. It was built in 1937. ($1-3)

St. Augustine Alligator Farm, 2008.

Over the past 115 years the St. Augustine Alligator Farm has been educating residents and visitors about prehistoric reptiles. People working at the farm are also continuously learning about these popular animals. Alligators, once housed in closed in areas that were no more than sand surrounded by a cement wall, now have free roam through marsh areas or exhibits specially designed to imitate their natural habitat. By imitating the natural habitat, the keepers are able to observe the mating and family interaction of the reptiles. After the boardwalk was constructed over a marsh containing many alligators, birds began stopping at the park during their migration with many nesting in the trees above the alligator infested water. The birds nest above the alligators knowing that they are safe from other predators that would harm their eggs, namely raccoons and opossums. Today, the Alligator Farm is much more than a collection of alligators. It is more of a zoo with numerous kinds of animals and bird life, in their natural habitat and several nature shows each day that dramatize the curious habits and activities of alligators, crocodiles and snakes. It also serves as a place for scientific research on the alligator and is one of the more important bird observation stations in the state.

St. Augustine Alligator Farm, Anastasia Island, 2008.

The St. Augustine Alligator Farm is one of the oldest attractions of its kind and, in recognition of its role in the development of tourism, has been placed on the National Register of Historic Places. Although the farm houses several thousand alligators and crocodiles, including representatives of all twenty-three species, it is more than just an Alligator Farm. It is also a zoological park. Other reptiles and monkeys can be seen, and egrets, wood storks, and herons nest above the alligator ponds.

Bibliography

Adams, William R. *St. Augustine & St. Johns County: A Historical Guide*. St. Augustine, Florida: Third Millennium Editions, 2005.

Adams, William R. and Paul L. Weaver, III. *Historical Places of St. Augustine and St. Johns County*. St. Augustine, Florida: Southern Heritage Press, 1993.

Arana, Luis Rafael and Albert Manucy. *The Building of Castillo de San Marcos*. St. Augustine, Florida: Eastern National Park & Monument Association, 1977.

Arana, Luis Rafael, Albert Manucy, and Jay Humphreys. *The History of Castillo de San Marcos*. St. Augustine, Florida: Historic Print & Map Company, 2005.

Arnade, Charles W. *The Siege of St. Augustine in 1702*. Gainesville, Florida: University of Florida Press, 1959.

Ayers, R. Wayne. *Florida's Grand Hotels from the Gilded Age*. Charleston, South Carolina: Arcadia Publishing, 2005.

Bierstadt, Edward. *Picturesque St. Augustine*. New York, New York: Artotype Publishing Company, 1891.

Boeschenstein, Warren. *Historic American Towns Along the Atlantic Coast*. Baltimore, Maryland: The John Hopkins University Press, 1999.

Bondy, Valerie C. *Florida Bed & Breakfast Guide*. Melbourne, Florida: Queen of Hearts Publications, 1995.

Bowen, Beth Rogero and the St. Augustine Historical Society. *St. Augustine in the Gilded Age*. Charleston, South Carolina: Arcadia Publishing, 2008.

Bruns, James H. *Great American Post Offices*. New York, New York: John Wiley & Sons, 1998.

Bryant, William C. *St. Augustine: A Guided Tour of America's Oldest City*. Picturesque America, 1872.

Chorlian, Meg, Editor. *St. Augustine: America's Oldest City*. Peterborough, New Hampshire: Cobblestone Publishing, Inc., 1995.

Colee, Schelia. *Historic Churches in St. Augustine*. St. Augustine, Florida: Self-published, 1984.

Dewhurst, William W. *The History of St. Augustine Florida*. New York, New York: G. P. Putnam's Sons, 1885.

Fort Matanzas. St. Augustine, Florida: National Park Service, 2002.

Fretwell, Jacquelin K, editor. *Civil War Times In St. Augustine*. Port Salerno, Florida: Florida Classics Library, 1988.

Frisbie, Louise K. *Florida's Fabled Inns*. Bartow, Florida: Imperial Publishing Company, 1980.

Graham, Thomas. *Flagler's Grand Hotel Alcazar*. St. Augustine, Florida: St. Augustine Historical Society, 1989.

Flagler's Magnificent Hotel Ponce de Leon. St. Augustine, Florida: St. Augustine Historical Society, 1975.

Flagler's St. Augustine Hotels. Sarasota, Florida: Pineapple Press, Inc., 2004.

St. Augustine, 1867. St. Augustine, Florida: St. Augustine Historical Society, 1996.

Green, Paul. *Cross and Sword, 1565-1965*. St. Augustine, Florida: St. Augustine's 400th Anniversary, Inc., 1965.

Gross, Steve and Sue Daley. *Old Florida: Florida's Magnificent Homes, Gardens, and Vintage Attractions*. New York, New York: Rizzoli International Publications, Inc., 2003.

Hall, Maggi Smith. *Flavors of St. Augustine*. Lake Buena Vista, Florida: Tailored Tours Publications, Inc., 1999.

Hall, Maggi Smith and the St. Augustine Historical Society. *St. Augustine*. Charleston, South Carolina: Arcadia Publishing, 2002.

Harvey, Karen. *St. Augustine and St. Johns County*. Virginia Beach, Virginia: Donning Company, Publishers, 1980.

Helfrick, Robb. *St. Augustine Impressions*. Helena, Montana: Farcountry Press, 2004.

Hiller, Herbert L. *Guide to the Small and Historic Lodgings of Florida*. Sarasota, Florida: Pineapple Press, Inc., 1988.

Historic Catholic Sites of St. Augustine. St. Augustine, Florida: Parish of the Cathedral of St. Augustine, 1988.

Laffal, Ken. *St. Augustine On My Mind*. Helena, Montana: Falcon Publishing Company, 2001.

Lee, W. Howard. *The Story of Old St. Augustine*. St. Augustine, Florida: Record Press, Inc., 1951.

Lidh, Rosalinda. *St. Augustine Lighthouse: A Short History*. St. Augustine, Florida: Historic Print & Map Company, 2004.

Manucy, Albert. *The Houses of St. Augustine: 1565-1821*. Gainesville, Florida: University Press of Florida, 1992.

Maynard, Charles W. *Castillo de San Marcos*. New York, New York: Rosen Publishing Group, Inc., 2002.

McCarthy, Kevin M. *Twenty Florida Pirates*. Sarasota, Florida: Pineapple Press, Inc., 1994.

Mulder, Kenneth W. *Piracy Days of Long Ago*. Tampa, Florida: Mulder Enterprises, 1995.

Nolan, David. *The Houses of St. Augustine*. Sarasota, Florida: Pineapple Press, 1995.

Peck, Douglas T. *Ponce de Leon and the Discovery of Florida*. Branden, Florida: Pogo Press, 1993

Pinkas, Lilly. *Guide to the Gardens of Florida*. Sarasota, Florida: Pineapple Press, Inc., 1998.

Potter, George L. *Authentic Biographies of the World's Greatest People*. St. Augustine, Florida: Potter's International Hall Of Fame, 1955.

Puckett, Ron, Rod Morris, and Mary Lou Phillips. *Yesterday in St. Augustine*. Tallahassee, Florida: Yesterday in Florida, Inc., 2003.

Rajtar, Steve and Kelly Goodman. *A Guide to Historic St. Augustine, Florida*. Charleston, South Carolina: The History Press, 2007.

Reese, Montana Lisle. *Bean Soup or Florida With a Spanish Accent*. Jacksonville, Florida: Crawford Publishing Company, 1964.

Reynolds, Charles B. *The Standard Guide: St. Augustine*. St. Augustine, Florida: Historic Print & Map Company, 2004.

Seeing St. Augustine. New York, New York: AMS Press Inc., 1937.

Spencer, Donald D. *Greetings from St. Augustine*. Atglen, Pennsylvania: Schiffer Publishing Ltd, 2008.

Steen, Sandra and Susan Steen. *Historic St. Augustine*. Parsippany, New Jersey: Dillon Press, 1997.

Stewart, Laura and Susanne Hupp. *Florida Historic Homes*. Orlando, Florida: Sentinel Communications Company, 1988.

Tellier, Mark. *St. Augustine's Pictures of the Past*. St. Augustine, Florida: Self-published, 1979.

Van Campen, J. T. *St. Augustine: Florida's Colonial Capital*. St. Augustine, Florida: St. Augustine Historical Society, 1959.

Voelbricht, John L. *St. Augustine's Historical Heritage As Seen Today*. St. Augustine, Florida: C. F. Hamblen, Inc., 1952.

Waterbury, Jean Parker. *St. Augustine Historical Society: Four Walking Tours*. St. Augustine, Florida: St. Augustine Historical Society, 2000.
   The Oldest City. St. Augustine, Florida: St. Augustine Historical Society, 1983.
   The Oldest House. St. Augustine, Florida: St. Augustine Historical Society, 1984.

Wiles, Jon W. *Invisible Saint Augustine*. St. Augustine, Florida: Self-published, 1994.

Wyllie, H. S. *St. Augustine Under Three Flags*. St. Augustine, Florida: Self-published, 1898.

St. Augustine Beach, Circa 1945.
Fishing enthusiasts enjoyed surf casting or fishing off the St. Johns County Pier, where their rewards of Spanish mackerel, amberjack, pompano, and sheep head could be measured by the pound. ($1-3)

St. Augustine Beach, 2008.
Beach activity at St. Augustine Beach centers on the St. Johns County Pier where visitors can fish and often watch dolphins and whales surfacing on top of the waves or surfers catching waves.

Index